Y0-BQH-896

Berlin · Schnitzler Bibliography 1965–1977

Jeffrey B. Berlin

An Annotated
Arthur Schnitzler Bibliography
1965–1977

With an Essay on The Meaning of the "Schnitzler-Renaissance"

Foreword by Sol Liptzin

Wilhelm Fink Verlag München

To
Anne
and
My Parents and Parents-in-law

ISBN 3-7705-1568-4
© 1978 Wilhelm Fink Verlag, München
Druck: Salzer, München
Buchbindearbeiten: Endres, München

Illustrations: Collection of Jeffrey B. Berlin

Table of Contents

PREFACE

The present bibliography includes primary and secondary material for the period of 1965 to 1977.

Annotations are given when deemed necessary. Detailed information on the contents of all Schnitzler dissertations (1917 to 1976) may be found in my previous Schnitzler bibliographies: see J. B. Berlin, *MAL*, 6, i/ii (1973), 7, i/ii (1974), 8, iii/iv (1975) and 9, ii (1976); space does not permit such detailed material to be included at the present time. *Any information pertaining to the bibliography (especially "Research in Progress") will be greatly appreciated.* It should be sent to J. B. Berlin, c/o Levy, 1135 Strahle Street, Philadelphia, Pa. 19111.

The following abbreviations are used throughout the bibliography:

AGR	American-German Review
BA	Books Abroad
DA	Dissertation Abstracts
DLZ	Deutsche Literatur Zeitung
EG	Etudes Germaniques
FH	Frankfurter Hefte
GL&L	German Life and Letters
GQ	German Quarterly
GR	Germanic Review
GRM	Germanisch-romanische Monatschrift
GW	Germanica Wratislaviensia
JEGP	Journal of English and Germanic Philology
JIASRA	Journal of the International Arthur Schnitzler Research Association
L&P	Literature & Psychology
LuK	Literatur und Kritik
MAL	Modern Austrian Literature
MLN	Modern Language Notes
MLQ	Modern Language Quarterly
MLR	Modern Language Review
MP	Modern Philology
MuK	Maske und Kothurn
NDH	Neue Deutsche Hefte
NZZ	Neue Zürcher Zeitung
ÖGL	Österreich in Geschichte und Literatur
RLV	Revue des Langues Vivantes
WW	Wirkendes Wort
ZDP	Zeitschrift für Deutsche Philologie

Finally, I wish to express my sincere appreciation to my many colleagues who generously sent me information or material on Schnitzler. I am especially grateful to the International Arthur Schnitzler Research Association and the State University of New York at Binghamton for their support of my Schnitzler projects during the past seven years. Also, Professor Heinrich Schnitzler, as well as Mrs. Miriam Beer-Hofmann Lens, Dr. Donald G. Daviau, Dr. Gerhard Köpf, Mrs. Elizabeth Levy, Dr. Hans-Ulrich Lindken, Dr. Sol Liptzin, Dr. Reinhard Urbach and Dr. Robert O. Weiss have been especially cooperative, helpful and generous of their time and knowledge, without which this study would have been impossible. To Mrs. Darragh Goodsite, editorial assistant for all journals at the State University of New York at Binghamton, I can only extend my most sincere thanks for much guidance and appreciated help. To Anne, my wife, I am most grateful for her patience, understanding and help.

FOREWORD

Arthur Schnitzler reached the height of his fame on the eve of the First World War. In 1912, his play *Professor Bernhardi* aroused tremendous interest both on the stage and in the printed version. The comments were not uniformly favorable but the controversy about the play's theme and conclusions had far flung journalistic and critical repercussions. In the same year, Otto Brahm, who had sparked the Schnitzler-vogue ever since the closing nineteenth century, died and Max Reinhardt, the most influential successor of Brahm among the Central European theater directors, was less enthusiastic about staging Schnitzler plays. With the outbreak of World War I and the rise of Expressionism in literature and art, Schnitzler's popularity began to recede. Although some of his best works appeared in the 1920's, he nevertheless came to be regarded as an historical rather than as a contemporary figure.

Schnitzler sensed the changing mood toward his subtle questionings, his overrefined rationalizations, his sceptical affirmations and his tired negations. Loneliness gathered about him during his final years and was reflected in his last works. He felt that he was no longer writing for his generation but rather for later ones. He expressed this feeling in his mellowest drama *Der Gang zum Weiher* (1927), when he wrote: "I speak to those who are to come. They alone are my friends. What disturbs you is that I am still alive. You are right. Our sojourn on earth falsifies our true being. Our life is a mask that clings to us. But when this mask is torn down, then whatever remains exists, not for us any longer but only for you."

These words proved to be prophetic. Interest in Schnitzler continued to recede as totalitarianism spread across Central Europe. His plays were not staged for more than a decade after 1933. He was all but forgotten during World War II. A generation after his death, however, a Schnitzler renaissance was in full swing and continued unabated throughout the 1960's and 1970's. Since 1961, the International Arthur Schnitzler Research Association stimulated Schnitzler studies through its meetings and its journal. In the same year, 1961, the most comprehensive edition of his works began to appear. Following the centennial of his birth, American scholars in 1963 issued a commemorative volume of important studies about him. His plays attracted ever wider audiences so that by 1974 Vienna's three largest theaters — Burgtheater, Volkstheater, Theater in der Josefstadt — were simultaneously staging his plays. Dissertations about various aspects of his works were being completed in European and American universities.

The present annotated bibliography, supplementing earlier ones, affords an insight into the Schnitzler vogue of the past decade and is an excellent reference work, paving the way for future research into the personality and creativity of this superb Austrian dramatist, narrator, and thinker.

February 24, 1977   Sol Liptzin

The Meaning of the "Schnitzler-Renaissance"

Jeffrey B. Berlin

Arthur Schnitzler's works, long subject to much misunderstanding and neglect, only recently have become fully appreciated and better received in the critical literature. Today Schnitzler has become the subject of growing interest and lively debate.[1] Almost all present studies have discarded the insupportable notion that Schnitzler's thematic range was severely limited, and topics such as fin de siècle Vienna, love and death or illusion versus reality are no longer considered his only themes. Similarly, it now is an accepted fact that Schnitzlerian characters constitute more than types, such as the "leichtsinniger Melancholiker" or "süsses Mädel." While *Anatol* or *Reigen, Liebelei* or *Der grüne Kakadu* are recognized as important, these works are no longer regarded as totally illustrative of Schnitzler's *oeuvre*, as critics once concluded.

Today's critical literature more effectively calls attention to the ideas and values within Schnitzler's art that make him representative of his times and his works applicable even to situations that contemporary man faces. The "Schnitzler-Renaissance"[2] began in the early 1960's. However, the change in the critical reception of Schnitzler evolved over a number of years. Several factors accentuated this "Schnitzler-Renaissance." Among these, the publication of the four-volume edition of Schnitzler's narrative and dramatic works by the S. Fischer Verlag in 1961-1962[3] represents a primary cause in directing attention toward Schnitzler. Before 1961 only scattered volumes of early editions were available. With the exception of a few books, his works were basically inaccessible, aside from anthologies that usually included standard works, such as *Anatol, Liebelei, Der blinde Geronimo* or *Der grüne Kakadu.*[4] Similarly, the formation by Robert O. Weiss of the International Arthur Schnitzler Research Association and the publication of a journal devoted to Schnitzler studies initiated increased activity in Schnitzler scholarship.[5] And recently, the publication of much previously unknown or unavailable material has greatly expanded the image of Schnitzler and almost completely altered the earlier sterotyped views of his works.[6] In particular, the efforts of Reinhard Urbach have been a tremendous aid to scholars concerned with Schnitzleriana.[7] Urbach's many editions of letters and his publication of dramatic fragments, aside from his editing numerous and diversified notes by Schnitzler, in addition to the important and well-received *Schnitzler-Kommentar,*[8] represent items that present day critics use daily in their work. Also, the unfailing and generous help afforded to scholars by Schnitzler's son, Professor

Heinrich Schnitzler (aside from his own well-documented editions, often co-edited by Therese Nickl) represents another primary factor in the increased quality and volume of material on Arthur Schnitzler. Additionally, the availability of Schnitzler's diaries and correspondences have served as increasingly important and revealing sources of information about Schnitzler and his era.[9] To be sure, it is necessary that the diaries in particular be consulted.[10] Perhaps it should be stated that they soon will be published after having been held up from publication, according to Schnitzler's own testimony,[11] many years.

Aside from this new material, however, the most significant changes in the criticism have been taken through the comprehending analyses and painstaking re-examinations of Schnitzler's works.[12] Among the areas studied is the mode of expression used by Schnitzler. No longer is it sufficient to comment that, for example, Schnitzler utilizes the indirect interior monologue, interior monologue, indirect dialogue or omniscient report of events and situations;[13] these devices must be explained — their function must be examined. At the same time, it is no longer sufficient to state that Schnitzler's works may be likened to those of Maupassant, Ibsen, Nietzsche, O'Neill or Genet, to name a few authors. Modern criticism demands that the areas of convergence or divergence be examined.[14] And other approaches to comparative criticism are also being written. The time of name dropping is past. Such comparative studies are not only interesting and necessary, but they represent areas that will never cease to attract attention, just as Schnitzler's works proper will ever remain challenging. Indeed, critics have finally discovered and begun to perceptively explain the *Weltanschauung* that Schnitzler maintained. Of course, there were occasional critics in the past (before 1961) who demonstrated a sound understanding of the Schnitzlerian work; but their number is few.[15]

Schnitzler's works discuss issues that man faces today and will face tomorrow. Loneliness and marriage, ethics and morality, deception and truth, to randomly cite a few examples, all represent problems[16] that run throughout his works. It is significant to realize, however, that these "problems" no longer are viewed merely as predominant thematic issues; rather, they are being subjected to full scale investigations, and their function and meaning are being explained in conjunction with Schnitzler's position on the particular subject.[17] And in another area, Schnitzler's grasp of psychology has become recognized as credible even when compared to Freudian or post-Freudian theories.[18] Today it may be flatly stated that the relationship between Freud and Schnitzler no longer ultimately rests upon the so-called "Doppelgänger" association.[19] Too much additional material substantiates Schnitzler's efforts and brilliant grasp of the dynamic structure of the psyche[20] to classify him as an admirer or imitator of Freud, with whom, incidentally, Schnitzler did not always agree.[21]

Critics are always interested in the genesis of a work. Thus, Schnitzler's works become all the more attractive. He maintained careful and scientific-type notes and only published a work when satisfied it met all the criteria of what he considered a respectable and good piece of literature. To give an example, one thinks of *Professor Bernhardi*, for which there are approximately 800 pages of draft material and notes.[22] Clearly Schnitzler's *Nachlaß* offers a rich abundance of material that awaits evaluation, editing and publication.[23] Of course, as early as 1931 Sol Liptzin, who personally knew Schnitzler and who had access to his material, presented three studies that discussed the genesis of *Der einsame Weg, Das weite Land* and *Professor Bernhardi*.[24] It is unfortunate that other scholars, with the exception of Otto P. Schinnerer,[25] did not follow Liptzin's pioneering efforts.

There are additional reasons for Schnitzler's "sudden" popularity. Certainly his works are now readily available. On the other hand, they are extremely appealing because, unlike some works of literature, Schnitzler's works may be read either for strict pleasure or for interpretation. They may serve a cathartic purpose or a scholarly function.[26] In both cases, the Schnitzlerian work is of particular interest to historians, sociologists, psychologists and literary critics, if one considers the more obvious professions.

One aspect cannot be forgotten: Schnitzler's religion caused him to suffer. His works were destroyed — some were burned. His *Nachlaß* was saved only because Eric Blackall, then a student at the University of Vienna, rescued it and carried it with him to England.[27] Despite efforts to suppress Jewish writers, Schnitzler has survived. And he has become recognized as a *Dichter* and *Denker*. As Reinhard Urbach so aptly expresses the point, "es bedarf keiner Rechtigung mehr, daß man das Werk Arthur Schnitzlers in den Vordergrund rückt, wenn von der deutschsprachigen Literatur zwischen 1890 und 1910 die Rede ist."[28] Correct as Urbach's remarks are, it must be remembered that Schnitzler's works are *not* time bound. His writings display universal situations: they paint a word picture of man, his surroundings and his response to such surroundings, as well as offering a unique portrayal with discerning clarity of Vienna at the turn of the century.[29] True, he suffered from a late start. But the steady interest continues to grow. The momentum cannot be stopped.

The forces that make the "Schnitzler-Renaissance" rest, of course, on the critics' powers of observation. Ultimately, however, the Schnitzlerian text is the most important factor. But the bibliographical apparatus, which this essay introduces, should not be overlooked. Critics are apt to follow past patterns. This becomes additionally troublesome when the criticism is both subjective and oftentimes unfounded or uncomprehending. The point is that critics can only avail themselves of what is available. And it takes a brave critic to reveal new theories. New ideas, however, will be found in much of the criticism for the period of 1965 to 1977. It can be expected that future criticism will be even more astute for two reasons: first, bibliographies now exist — critics are aware of all of the criticism; and, second, for the reasons cited, Schnitzler's works are being studied by a more discerning eye.

Before presenting the bibliography, let us very briefly discuss Richard Allen's contribution that represented the long awaited breakthrough to Schnitzler scholars everywhere. True, there have been many reviews of the published version of his bibliography, but no one has offered a critique of the dissertation from which his book stems[30] and which serves as a *Forschungsbericht* for the period 1894 to 1964. In fact, Richard Allen's 1964 University of Michigan dissertation is clearly one of the most significant advancements for Schnitzler scholarship. While any bibliography is usually welcomed, Allen's annotated bibliography was not only helpful, but urgently needed. Before its publication there existed no such reference tool for Schnitzler studies, [31] and many a person overlooked significant material simply because it was not easily located or virtually impossible to uncover during the course of any one study.

As noted, his dissertation proper is generally assumed to be the equivalent of the published bibliography — an assumption that is grossly incorrect. It is indeed regrettable that the published edition could not include the section of his dissertation that discussed at length the critical reception of Schnitzler's works. Although the annotations in the book version are of extreme help, it is very advantageous to have the full study readily available. All in all, however, the dissertation represents the first thorough examination of Schnitzler's critical reception.

Allen's approach is specifically outlined in the introduction to his work, and he accomplishes his goal admirably. The study proper is divided into three major areas: 1) Arthur Schnitzler's life and works; 2) the critical reception of Schnitzler's works; and 3) the bibliography. The second section is carefully subdivided into the following categories: a) criticism through 1912; b) criticism from 1913 through 1922; c) criticism from 1923 through 1932; and d) criticism from 1933 to the present, which, for Allen, was 1963. (The published version includes some of the criticism for 1965).

In his introduction Allen establishes the state of Schnitzler scholarship and notes the bibliographical status of Schnitzler research then. As he indicates, no bibliographies existed, with the exception of Schinnerer's that was begun in 1932 but never completed. A brief discussion of Schnitzler's published writings is also covered in the introductory section.

In the first chapter Allen presents a helpful biographical sketch of Schnitzler's life. Considering when Allen prepared his work, this section proves to be quite adequate, although it could now be greatly expanded in view of recently discovered and published material. But Allen's lack of detail is not attributable to his inability to uncover the facts. He presents the basic information and satisfactorily summarizes the essential points. Without

4

doubt, his treatment is conscientiously prepared, and he drew upon all available information.

In chapter two, Allen traces the reactions of the critics to Schnitzler's works. To be sure, Allen is careful in his selection of those critics whose studies he examines; his presentation is thorough and not limited or subjective. At all times he deals with the facts. His discussion surely answers the question of what contributions Schnitzler critics have made concerning Schnitzler's works.

Chapter three comprises the bibliography that is exhaustive in scope. As reviewers have shown,[32] in general few errors are to be found.[33] Schnitzler's works are chronologically listed first in the original German publications and then English translations are presented, again in chronological order. After this a listing of Schnitzler's works that have been translated into French is presented. Next follows a chronological listing of the criticism on Schnitzler. Before an index of personal names, a section entitled subject index and reviews is presented.

The conclusions that Allen draws are valid and based on objectively analyzed evidence. He notes, for example: "While the earliest criticism was rather superficial, the second period of Schnitzler studies, 1913-1923, saw a greater critical discernment and culminated in the monographs by Roseeu and especially Körner."[34] Allen continues by maintaining: "between 1923 and 1931 Schnitzler scholarship was established with Schinnerer as the leading contributor. In general, attention turned from the dramas to the narratives, Körner stressing that the late Novellen represent a contribution of Schnitzler's development. . . . Schinnerer's studies marked the beginning of biographical and bibliographical investigations of the writer."[35] Finally, Allen observes that "Schnitzler criticism since 1933 has been surprising in its variety and volume. Generally speaking, the clichés of "old Vienna" and das süsse Mädel have given way to more incisive analysis. Taking up Körner's suggestions, scholars like Blume, Plaut, and Seidlin examined the author's nihilism and primitivism, and such basic structural devices as the Umbruch with remarkable success."[36]

In conclusion, then, Allen's comments are self-explanatory: "To characterize the development of Schnitzler criticism, one might say that the author's image has changed from that of the gay yet melancholy Anatol of the earlier works to that of a much more problematic Casanova type of his later narratives and dramas. Schnitzler criticism has moved from an adulation of the youthful author of witty dialogues to an appreciation of the totality of his accomplishment."[37]

With the publication in 1966 of the bibliography proper, scholars were at long last offered the valuable tool they needed. Allen showed himself to be a competent and meticulously careful bibliographer. However, Allen has since left the field of Germanistik,[38] and it seems doubtful that commentary in his

5

dissertation will ever become accessible except in its present format. Clearly it warrants reading and discussion, and it should become a standard reference work, even if it must be obtained as a dissertation.

In December of 1976 Herbert Seidler's publication "Die Forschung zu Arthur Schnitzler seit 1945" appeared in the *Zeitschrift für Deutsche Philologie*.[39] To be sure, it is of the finest scholarly caliber and offers a sound critique of Schnitzler research. Without question, it perceptively introduces the student and scholar alike to Schnitzleriana. At the same time, Seidler is too erudite to ignore the early critics, and he appropriately cites the major studies that appeared before 1945 and thus expands the scope of his discussion. While the books that he analyzes have been reviewed, few have been examined in the terse and masterly manner that Seidler displays. The same may be said of his approach to the articles, although with them he keeps his discussion minimal, as would be expected. The study itself is divided into seven categories: "1. Bibliographien und Forschungsberichte; 2. Ausgaben; 3. Allgemeine Darstellungen; 4. Zum Leben; 5. Besondere Sichten auf das ganze Schaffen; 6. Das dramatische Werk; 7. Das erzählerische Werk."

To be sure, no summary can do justice either to Allen's dissertation or Seidler's *Forschungsbericht*. Because Seidler's study is available in all major libraries, it undoubtedly will be consulted by conscientious critics. It not only saves one much time by providing the proper scholarly "atmosphere," but also contains many valuable observations that can only be presented after much examination of Schnitzler and his critics.

In the same year, this writer also prepared a survey of Schnitzler scholarship, and the work is forthcoming in book form, although it is presently available in dissertation form.[40] Unlike Seidler's approach, here a year by year summarization of the majority of critical studies on Schnitzler for the period of 1965 to 1975 is offered. In this way, the reader is readily able to ascertain if a specific study is relevant to his own project. With the understanding that a brief summary cannot do justice to all aspects of the work being examined, it can safely be stated such an approach does allow the critic to become aware of the basic thematic content of the work under discussion. All studies are by necessity not examined, and my work does have, like Seidler's, certain restrictions and limitations. However, only the minor studies are eliminated. Thus, both Seidler's and my survey have similar goals, even though our approaches are entirely different. But these acknowledged factors do not detract from our stated purpose: namely, to establish the trend that Schnitzler scholarship has taken over the past years.

Much more needs to be written about the development of Schnitzler criticism. Such scholarship has now reached the level at which reviews of all of the studies dealing with a particular narrative or dramatic work could and should be written. *Traumnovelle* or *Professor Bernhardi*, *Der Weg ins Freie* or *Anatol*, *Fräulein Else* or *Der grüne Kakadu* all have been extensively treated in the critical literature. The same may be said of many other Schnitzlerian works, and it is time to evaluate the criticism and to develop a clear understanding as to where we stand on a particular work. It is hoped that the present bibliography, which offers the primary and secondary material in an organized manner and which serves as a sequel to Allen's work, will stimulate further discussion and result in even more studies over the next ten year period.

NOTES

1. There are various studies that substantiate this statement. One immediately thinks of Reinhard Urbach's important evaluation of the edition of *Das Wort*. Above all, he shows how necessary it is to consider, with great precision and accuracy, *all* of the materials about a particular work. See: Reinhard Urbach, "Schwätzer sind Verbrecher: Bemerkungen zu Schnitzlers Dramenfragment 'Das Wort'," *Literatur und Kritik*, 25 (1968), 292-304.

    In another area, it has long been argued if *Professor Bernhardi* is a "Tendenzstück." Critics are divided in their positions, despite Schnitzler's supposedly clear statement about the work: "Ich habe eine Charakterkomödie geschrieben, die in ärztlichen und zum Teil in politischen Kreisen spielt, kein Tendenzstück, das den Konflikt zwischen Wissenschaft und Kirche oder gar, wie Sie meinen, den Streit zwischen Religionen darzustellen oder am Ende in irgendeiner Richtung zu entscheiden sucht" (in: letter of January 4, 1913 to Richard Charmatz. Reproduced in Siegfried Melchinger, "Das Jüdische in 'Professor Bernhardi'," *Theater heute*, 5, xii [1964] 32-33). At the same time, critics are uncertain if the work is, in fact, a comedy. See William H. Rey, *Arthur Schnitzler. Professor Bernhardi* (München: Wilhelm Fink Verlag, 1971). These problems are complicated by the fact that the validity of Schnitzler's own statements must remain in question. We know that Schnitzler flatly denied that the figure of Professor Bernhardi was modeled after his father or the Elisabethinum after his father's Poliklinik (in: letter of February 27, 1913 to Georg Brandes. *Georg Brandes/ Arthur Schnitzler. Ein Briefwechsel,* ed. Kurt Bergel [Bern: Francke Verlag, 1956], p. 106). Yet, in an early draft of *Professor Bernhardi* Schnitzler refers to the hospital by the name of the "Poliklinik," not "Elisabethinum" (Arthur Schnitzler, *Nachlaß*, Reel 114, File 117: section entitled "Ärtztestück," p. 3. Consulted with permission of the International Arthur Schnitzler Research Association at the State University of New York at Binghamton, where the microfilms are housed). As the manuscript reveals, the first time that Schnitzler mentions the name of the hospital he seems to be aware of his error and has a marginal note indicating that the name should be changed from "Poliklinik" to "Elisabethinum." Later, when the necessity of giving a name to the hospital arises, Schnitzler simply reverts back to his model hospital and the name "Poliklinik" again appears in the manuscript. Surely, it seems, this information, as well as other supporting material, suggests that the work is partially autobiographical (additional information in: Jeffrey B. Berlin, "The Treatment of Truth in the Dramatic Work of Henrik Ibsen and Arthur Schnitzler," Ph.D. Diss. State University of New York at Binghamton, pp. 413-415. Summary in: Dissertation

Abstracts, 37, iii [1976], p. 1576 A).

Thus, much study of *Professor Bernhardi* is justified. Similar discussions are warranted for his other works.

2. Basic studies that illustrate the modern trend in Schnitzler criticism are the following: Frederick J. Beharriell, "Arthur Schnitzler's Range of Theme," *Monatshefte*, 43, vii (1951), 301-311; William H. Rey, "Arthur Schnitzler," in: *Deutsche Dichter der Moderne*, ed. Benno von Wiese, 3rd ed. (Berlin: Erich Schmidt Verlag, 1975), pp. 247-269; Reinhard Urbach, *Schnitzler* 2nd ed. (Velber bei Hannover: Friedrich Verlag, 1972), 143 p. (English translation: *Schnitzler* (New York: Frederick Ungar Publishing Co., 1973), 202 p.); and, Robert O. Weiss, "Arthur Schnitzler's Literary and Philosophical Development," *Journal of the International Arthur Schnitzler Research Association*, 2, i (1963), 4-20.

3. Arthur Schnitzler, *Gesammelte Werke: Die erzählenden Schriften*. 2 vols. (Frankfurt a.M.: S. Fischer Verlag, 1961). Arthur Schnitzler, *Gesammelte Werke: Die dramatischen Werke*. 2 vols. (Frankfurt a.M.: S. Fischer Verlag, 1962). See also, Arthur Schnitzler, *Gesammelte Werke: Aphorismen und Betrachtungen*. Ed. Robert O. Weiss (Frankfurt a.M.: S. Fischer Verlag, 1967) and Arthur Schnitzler, *Gesammelte Werke: Entworfenes und Verworfenes. Aus dem Nachlaß*. Ed. Reinhard Urbach (Frankfurt a.M.: S. Fischer Verlag, 1977).

4. This unavailability obviously impeded Schnitzler studies. Thus, it is not surprising to find the following comments introducing the dissertation of H. S. Reiss: "Owing to the present circumstances I found it impossible to procure all the books and magazines containing appreciations of Schnitzler and his work and I also was unable to study a few of his minor publications." He further observes: "Any work on Arthur Schnitzler must be incomplete, as his manuscripts, containing unpublished works, sketches and plans of plays, novels and stories, diaries, his letters and last not least his autobiography are not accessible at the moment." In: H. S. Reiss, "The Work of Arthur Schnitzler," Ph.D. Diss. University of Dublin, 1945, p. i.

5. Weiss' comments in the first issue of the journal are significant: "Because of certain difficulties involved in gaining access to it [the *Nachlaß*], few scholars have worked with this material thus far. The IASRA now provides for qualified scholars much more convenient ways of consulting reproductions of the posthumous papers and will also maintain a co-ordination and consultation service to facilitate research." Weiss further observes: "To lift the treasure of Schnitzler's work, to obtain for it its rightful place among the great cultural accomplishments of modern times, it is also essential that a central organi-

zation exist that may receive and disburse the funds required not only to stimulate or finance the desirable research, but also to make it possible for scholars concerned to have the results of their work published." In: Robert O. Weiss, "Why an International Arthur Schnitzler Research Association? ," *Journal of the International Arthur Schnitzler Research Association,* 1, i (1961), 4. In 1968 the title of the journal was changed to *Modern Austrian Literature.*

6. For a catalogue of the *Nachlaß* papers see: Gerhard Neumann and Jutta Müller, *Der Nachlaß Arthur Schnitzlers* (München: Wilhelm Fink Verlag, 1969).

7. An interesting example is the article by Theodor W. Alexander, "Olga Waissnix: The Model for the Character of the Married Woman in the Early Works of Arthur Schnitzler" (in: *Modern Austrian Literature,* 7, i/ii [1974], 99-107). The article is based on the correspondence between Olga Waissnix and Schnitzler that comprises letters written between 1886 and 1897. Clearly his study could not have been prepared without this correspondence.

8. Reinhard Urbach, *Schnitzler-Kommentar zu den erzählenden Schriften und dramatischen Werken* (München: Winkler Verlag, 1974). Without question, the *Schnitzler-Kommentar* will long be regarded as a basic reference work on Schnitzler. Each of its sections contains an enormous wealth of factual information which, in most cases, was hitherto unknown or unavailable to Schnitzler critics. The bulk of the book is devoted to the commentary on the 58 narrative and 39 dramatic works that comprise Schnitzler's published *oeuvre* in the 1961/62 S. Fischer edition. The seventy-page introduction, however, should not be overlooked. Here too, Urbach exhibits his expertise and provides us with an orderly and concise sketch of Schnitzler's life and times, often basing his facts on information in Schnitzler's diaries. For the Schnitzler specialist Urbach presents a handy reference work that is loaded with new information. For the student and teacher the book may well go hand in hand with classroom work and also help to clarify some of the more difficult expressions while, at the same time, quickly suggesting which studies may be most beneficial for future Schnitzler study.

9. Schnitzler kept diaries for the period of 1879 to 1931. The original drafts are housed at the Schiller-Nationalmuseum in Marbach am Neckar, Germany and may be consulted with special permission. The diaries soon will be published under the editorship of Reinhard Urbach, in cooperation with Heinrich Schnitzler.

10. The diaries comprise approximately 5000 typewritten pages. Baumann characterizes them well: "In ihm breitet sich die Schnitzler-Welt aus — Erfahrungen und Ueberlegungen, die eine Weltepoche in persönlichen

Einstellungen reflektieren und summieren − Erörterungen, die über das Individuelle hinausweisen, selbst wenn sie von persönlichen Anliegen handeln, dem Allgemeinen wiederum eine individuelle Physiognomie verleihen. Das Miteinander von Alltäglichem und Beispiellosem verknüpft sich mit den Jahren zunehmend Dichter. Ueberlieferungen und Begebenheiten, Urteile und Entwürfe − sie bilden eine Welt, die ihren Bezugspunkt in Arthur Schnitzler nie verleugnet; da er jedoch so vieles und Verschiedenartiges auf sich zu beziehen vermag, erreicht sie eine erregende Spannweite und Anziehungskraft − eine Welt, die den Leser für sich einnimmt, weil sie ihm einen weiten Spielraum eröffnet." in: Gerhart Baumann, "Arthur Schnitzlers Tagebücher. Eine Welt in Tagen − Jahrzehnte einer Welt," *Neue Zürcher Zeitung*, Nr. 230, Oktober 4/5 (1975), 59. See also: Karin Kathrein, "Schnitzler: Welt in Tagebüchern. 5000 Seiten warten auf Entdeckung," *Die Presse* [Wien], (Dec. 24, 1975), 7; and see the article by Gerhard Baumann in this issue.

11. Cf. Schnitzler's statement about his diaries. In: letter of August 16, 1918. Reproduced in Gerhard Neumann and Jutta Müller *Der Nachlaß Arthur Schnitzlers* (München: Wilhelm Fink Verlag, 1969), p. 33.

12. See, for example: J. B. Berlin, "The Element of 'Hope' in Arthur Schnitzler's *Sterben*," *Seminar. A Journal of Germanic Studies*, 10, i (1974), 38-49; and, by the same author, "Political Criticism in Arthur Schnitzler's *Aphorismen und Betrachtungen*," *Neophilologus*, 57, ii (1973), 173-178; Jon D. Green, "Musical Structure and Meaning in Arthur Schnitzler's *Zwischenspiel*," *Modern Austrian Literature*, 6, i/ii (1973), 7-25; Ernst L. Offermanns, *Arthur Schnitzler. Das Komödienwerk als Kritik des Impressionismus* (München: Wilhelm Fink Verlag, 1973), 244 p.; William H. Rey, *Arthur Schnitzler: Die späte Prosa als Gipfel seines Schaffens* (Berlin: Erich Schmidt Verlag, 1968), 198 p.; Hartmut Scheible, *Arthur Schnitzler in Selbstzeugnissen und Bildokumenten* (Reinbek bei Hamburg: Rowohlt Taschenbuch Verlag GmbH, 1976), 157 p.; Kenneth Segar, "Determinism and Character: Arthur Schnitzler's *Traumnovelle* and his Unpublished Critique of Psychoanalysis," *Oxford German Studies*, 8 (1973), 114-127; Martin Swales, *Arthur Schnitzler: A Critical Study* (London: Oxford University Press, 1971), 289 p.; Robert O. Weiss, "The Human Element in Arthur Schnitzler's Social Criticism," *Modern Austrian Literature*, 5, i/ii (1972), 30-44.

13. One of the finest studies available on this topic is by Maria D. Reid. See Maria D. Reid, "Aspects of Theme and Technique in Arthur Schnitzler's Shorter Prose Fiction," Ph.D. Diss. University of California at Los Angeles, 1969. Summary in: Dissertation Abstracts, 30, viii (1970), 3473-3474 A.

14. Let us offer a very brief example by considering Ibsen and Schnitzler. To begin, Schnitzler's works have many distinguishing characteristics that suggest he was influenced by Ibsen. Indeed, Schnitzler has often been called the "Austrian Ibsen," a term that may justifiably be accepted provided one realizes that Schnitzler's works are highly original and not imitations of any Ibsenian work. Thematically speaking, several of Ibsen's ideas find their way into his works, but this may also be due to the cross-current of thinking at the time. In a sense, Schnitzler is a moralist, but he does not manipulate characters to convey his own position. Unlike Ibsen, Schnitzler's characters seem more free and less limited in their ability to live their own lives. Ibsen's characters are not conceived in any mathematical formulation, but they do seem less able to respond to life than are Schnitzler's characters. Perhaps this is because the Schnitzlerian character is no longer fighting against lies and hypocrisy; he simply accepts it as part of life and lives accordingly. With Ibsen, men such as Thomas and Peter Stockman, Gregers Werle or Brand are determined to obtain their own way. Schnitzler's characters, on the other hand, seem more relaxed, even though they suffer greatly from problems that are equally as tragic as the ones that Ibsen depicts.

More specifically, each author was greatly concerned about truth, and their attitudes towards the truth problem appear to be in agreement: there exists no absolute truth. Although some of their characters seek it, they are only frustrated in their efforts to achieve it. But in their attempt to achieve absolute truth — or simply truth itself — rests the difference between the Austrian Schnitzler and the Norwegian Ibsen. Ibsen's works continually appear as if he had a moral to preach; although Schnitzler's works are not without a moral, they clearly are not as dogmatically expressed as are Ibsen's views. Further, Ibsen employs much symbolism to express his convictions; such symbolism, dramatically speaking, is extremely effective and greatly adds to the excellence of his works. But within the implicit meaning of the symbol can often be discovered Ibsen's message. He realizes that certain expressions cannot be achieved with mere words, and thus he resorts to symbols to clarify his point. Symbolism exists in Schnitzler works also, but certainly not to the extent that Ibsen employs it.

Each author is concerned with man, and their fight for the individual to allow himself to retain his free will and God given rights is interesting to compare. Ibsen stresses that often an outsider is needed to coach another individual into the right position, yet each time such help enters the field there follows chaos and moral disaster. Ibsen attempts again and again to help his characters, but this idealistic viewpoint cannot be permitted for the characters refuse to accept such intrusions. Schnitzler, on the other hand, allows his characters to speak for themselves. They seem to behave more naturally, almost as if they were simply gliding along the waters of life without an end in sight.

Needless to say, the above only represents one aspect of the relationship between Ibsen and Schnitzler. And, at that, there are many other areas that need to be discussed. However, the point is that such comparative studies offer a rich abundance of material for examination. (The problem of influences on Schnitzler must remain a thorny area: cf. Haskell M. Block, "The Concept of Influence in Comparative Literature," *Yearbook of Comparative and General Literature*, 7 (1958), pp. 30-37).

15.   See, for example: Alfred Apsler, "A Sociological View of Arthur Schnitzler," *Germanic Review*, 18, ii (1943), 90-106; Selma Koehler, "The Question of Moral Responsibility in the Dramatic Works of Arthur Schnitzler," *Journal of English and Germanic Philology*, 22, iii (1923), 376-411; Josef Körner, *Arthur Schnitzlers Gestalten und Probleme* (Wien: Amalthea, 1921); Herbert Lederer, "Arthur Schnitzler: A Chronicle of Loneliness," *German Quarterly*, 30, ii (1957), 82-94; Sol Liptzin, *Arthur Schnitzler* (New York: Prentice Hall, 1932); Theodor Reik, *Arthur Schnitzler als Psycholog* (Minden, Westfalen: J.C.C. Bruns, 1913); Otto P. Schinnerer, "The Early Works of Arthur Schnitzler," *Germanic Review*, 4, ii (1929), 153-197; and, by the same author: "The Literary Apprenticeship of Arthur Schnitzler," *Germanic Review*, 5, i (1930), 58-82. "Introduction," in: Viennese Novelettes (New York: Simon & Schuster, 1931), pp. vii-xlv; and, Richard Specht, *Arthur Schnitzler: Der Dichter und sein Werk* (Berlin: S. Fischer, 1922).

16.   It is significant to realize that Schnitzler was not writing about problems: In the *Aphorismen und Betrachtungen* (p. 103) he commented: "Niemals ist es das Problem, das du gewählt, niemals der Geist, mit dem du es behandelt, was dein Werk in die Zukunft tragen wird; immer sind es nur die Gestalten, die du gebildet und die Atmosphäre, die du rings um sie geschaffen." He further observed (p. 473): "In einem Kunstwerk handelt es sich nie um ein Problem an sich, sondern immer nur um das Schicksal des Problems in einer Gestalt, es gibt daher im ästhetischen Sinn keine alten und keine neuen Probleme. Es gibt daher auch keine neuen und alten Gestalten, sondern nur wahre und unwahre Gestalten." And in a letter to Josef Körner he expressed: "Es handelt sich ja in der Kunst . . . überhaupt a priori nicht um Probleme, sondern immer nur um Gestalten" (letter of July 11, 1927 in: Evan B. Davis, "Moral Problems in the Works of Arthur Schnitzler," Ph.D. Diss. University of Pennsylvania [1950], p. 187). Schnitzler was an explorer

of the suffering mind. The topics of which he wrote tell of the reasons and causes for man's suffering. Schnitzler sought out some of the causes and effects of man's unhappiness, but it remained the individual that always interested him — *not* the problem proper.

17. See, for example: Albert Deneve, "Emblem of the Human Spirit: Arthur Schnitzler's *Der Geist im Wort und der Geist in der Tat*," Ph.D. Diss. State University of New York at Binghamton, 1976. Summary in: Dissertation Abstracts, 36, xii (1976), 8084 A; and, Klaus Kilian, *Die Komödien Arthur Schnitzlers. Sozialer Rollenzwang und kritische Ethik* (Düsseldorf: Verlagsgruppe Bertelsmann GmbH, 1972).

18. Cf. the valuable study by Robert O. Weiss: "A Study of Arthur Schnitzler (with Special Consideration of the problem of Psychosis in *Flight into Darkness* Ph.D. Diss. Stanford University, 1955. It may be noted that this study contains a lengthy introduction that takes into account many of the basic and fundamental issues about Schnitzler.

19. See Frederick J. Beharriell, "Freud's 'Double:' Arthur Schnitzler," *Journal of the American Psychoanalytic Association*, 10, iv (1962), 722-730 and also, Bernd Urban, "Arthur Schnitzler und Sigmund Freud: Aus den Anfängen des 'Doppelgängers.' Zur Differenzierung dichterischer Intuition und Umgebung der frühen Hysterieforschung," *Germanisch-Romanische Monatsschrift*, 24, ii (1974), 193-223.

20. See above, note 18.

21. Dr. Reinhard Urbach expressed this point during a lecture he presented at Syracuse University, Syracuse, New York on October 1, 1974.

22. Consulted with permission of the International Arthur Schnitzler Research Association at the State University of New York at Binghamton, where the microfilm reels are housed.

23. A good example is Rena Schlein's recent publication. See Arthur Schnitzler, *Ritterlichkeit, Fragment aus dem Nachlaß*, ed. Rena Schlein (Bonn: Bouvier Verlag Herbert Grundmann, 1975).

24. Presently I am editing the correspondence between Liptzin and Schnitzler. It dates from 1929 to 1931.

See Sol Liptzin, "The Genesis of Schnitzler's *Der einsame Weg*," *Journal of English and Germanic Philology*, 30, iii (1931), 392-404; and, by the same author, "The Genesis of Schnitzler's *Professor Bernhardi*," *Philological Quarterly*, 10, iv (1931), 348-355; and, "The Genesis of Schnitzler's *Das weite Land*," *Publications of the Modern Language Association*, 46, iii (1931), 860-866.

25. Presently I am editing the correspondence between Schinnerer and Schnitzler. It dates from 1928 to 1931.

26. Cf. Weiss, "The Human Element in Schnitzler's Social Criticism," *Modern Austrian Literature*, 5, i/ii (1972), 30.

27. See Otto P. Schinnerer, "Arthur Schnitzler's 'Nachlaß'," *Germanic Review*, 8, ii (1933), 114-123; and, Gerhard Neumann and Jutta Müller, *Der Nachlaß Arthur Schnitzlers* (München: Wilhelm Fink Verlag, 1969).

28. Reinhard Urbach, *Schnitzler-Kommentar zu den erzählenden Schriften und dramatischen Werken* (München: Winkler Verlag, 1974), p. 7.

29. Cf. Robert A. Kann, "The Image of the Austrian in Arthur Schnitzler's Work," in: *Studies in Arthur Schnitzler*, ed. Herbert W. Reichert and Herman Salinger (Chapel Hill: University of North Carolina Press, 1963), pp. 45-70.

30. Richard H. Allen, "Arthur Schnitzler's Works and their Reception: An Annotated Bibliography," Ph.D. Diss. University of Michigan, 1964. Richard H. Allen, *An Annotated Arthur Schnitzler Bibliography. Editions and Criticism in German, French, and English 1879-1965* (Chapel Hill: University of North Carolina Press, 1966).

31. The bibliographies that were available were either out-of-date or incomplete. In 1913 Archibald Henderson published a study entitled "Arthur Schnitzler (1862-   ): A Bibliography. Translations, Productions and Criticism in English," which appeared in the *Bulletin of Bibliography and Quarterly Dramatic Index*, 7, vii (1913), 155-156. In 1937 Georg Nussbaum prepared a 132 page dissertation at the University of Vienna entitled "Die Aufnahme Schnitzlers bei Kritik und Publikum." His work is no longer in the library and possibly was destroyed or lost during the war. All efforts to locate Dr. Nussbaum have thus far been unsuccessful. In 1932, however, Otto P. Schinnerer had published four of an intended nine sections of his bibliography, but this did not include criticism. In: Otto P. Schinnerer, "Systematisches Verzeichnis der Werke von Arthur Schnitzler," *Jahrbuch deutscher Bibliophilen und Literaturfreude*, 18/19 (1932-1933), 94-121.

Schnitzler most likely was concerned with such bibliographical data, as he not only kept careful records of where his works appeared, but also sometimes even aided scholars. For example, in his letter of January 9, 1929 to Schinnerer, he responds to several bibliographical questions. Of more significance is a bibliography prepared by E. Metalmann of *Die neue Literatur*. Apparently Metalmann was intending to publish a bibliography, for he had sent the original to Schinnerer and copies to both the S. Fischer Verlag and to Arthur Schnitzler, as a letter dated February 18, 1932 to Professor Heinrich Schnitzler reveals. As Metalmann indicates, Arthur Schnitzler had checked his bibliography and made some additions and corrections. Why his work never appeared is still unknown. Schnitzler's correspondence with Schinnerer does not mention the Metalmann bibliography.

Two other helpful studies existed, each of which was written under the direction of Professor Schinnerer of Columbia University.

These are: 1) Lawrence E. Gemeinhart, "The Reception of Arthur Schnitzler in Berlin, 1895-1914," M. A. Thesis, Columbia University (1931), 56 p.; and 2) Beatrice M. Schrumpf, "The Reception of Arthur Schnitzler in the United States," M. A. Thesis, Columbia University (1931), 53 p. Each of these theses contain fairly complete bibliographies for material pertinent to their respective topic. Schnitzler, in fact, was impressed with Schrumpf's study, as he notes in a letter dated April 11, 1931 to Schinnerer: "Ich weiss nicht, ob ich Ihnen schon gesagt habe, wie vorzüglich und wie fleissig gemacht ich die bibliographische Arbeit der Miss Schrumpf gefunden habe. Uebringens habe ich ihr persönlich selbstverständlich schon gedankt." (I am presently editing all of Arthur Schnitzler's still unpublished letters to his publishers, agents, translators and critics in the United States. This project, of course, includes Schnitzler's letters to Schinnerer. This material has been made available to me by Professor Heinrich Schnitzler, and I wish at this time to express my sincere appreciation to him for access to these letters. I also wish to thank Dr. Reinhard Urbach who first suggested the project and who has been extremely helpful.)

Aside from the above noted studies, scholars were dependent upon bibliographies usually contained in dissertations. Few books on Schnitzler were available, and those that existed did not contain bibliographies that were of much value. Accordingly, Allen's work was welcomed.

32. See item H27 of the bibliography.
33. While criticism of Allen's bibliography has been extremely favorable, some errors have been noted. In particular see the review by Reinhard Urbach in: *Literatur und Kritik*, 15 (1967), 324-328; see also, Jeffrey B. Berlin, " 'Forgotten' Schnitzler Dissertations," *Modern Austrian Literature*, 3, iv (1970), 68; and, by the same author, "Arthur Schnitzler Bibliography for 1974-1975," *Modern Austrian Literature*, 8, iii/iv (1975), 248-249.
34. Richard Harry Allen, "Arthur Schnitzler's Works and Their Reception: An Annotated Bibliography," Diss. University of Michigan (1964), p. 80.
35. *Ibid.*, p. 81.
36. *Ibid.*, p. 82.
37. *Ibid.*, p. 83.
38. Presently Dr. Allen is director of The Beatrice Public Library in Beatrice, Nebraska.
39. Vol. 95, no. iv (1976), 567-595.
40. Appendex B. A Survey of Scholarship on Schnitzler: 1965-1975, in: J. B. Berlin, The Treatment of Truth in The Dramatic Work of Henrik

Ibsen and Arthur Schnitzler. Diss. State University of New York at Binghamton, 1976, pp. 473-596. Available on demand from: Xerox University Microfilms 300 North Zeeb Road, Ann Arbor, Michigan, 48106.

A. *Primary Literature: Narrative Works*

1967

A1 SCHNITZLER, ARTHUR: *Kriegsgeschichte.* Ed. Reinhard Urbach. In: LuK, 13 (1967), 133-134.

A2 —————: *Roman-Fragment.* Ed. Reinhard Urbach. In: LuK, 13 (1967), 137-181.

1968

A3 SCHNITZLER, ARTHUR: *Novelette.* In: Almanach. Das zweiundachtzigste Jahr. Frankfurt a.M.: S. Fischer Verlag, 1968, pp. 53-61.

1969

A4 SCHNITZLER, ARTHUR: *Der Weg ins Freie. Frühere Pläne.* In: Giuseppe Farese, Individuo e societa nel romanzo "Der Weg ins Freie" di Arthur Schnitzler. Rome: Bulzoni, 1969, pp. 89-221.

1971

A5 SCHNITZLER, ARTHUR: *Aus Arthur Schnitzlers Werkstatt. Unveröffentlichte Entwürfe und Szenen.* In: NZZ, Nr. 25, January 17, 1971.

B. *Primary Literature: Dramatic Works*

1966

B1 SCHNITZLER, ARTHUR: *Das Wort.* Ed. Kurt Bergel. Frankfurt a.M.: S. Fischer Verlag, 1966, 150 p.
Reviewed by:
B1.1 Farese, Giuseppe. In: Studi Germanici, 5, i (1967), 95-100.
B1.2 Illing, Hans. In: JIASRA, 6, ii (1967), 41-43.

1968

B2 SCHNITZLER, ARTHUR: *Aus den Vorarbeiten zu "Liebelei".* In: Neue Blätter des Theaters in der Josefstadt. 1968/1969. [Sketch dated Dec. 13, 1893].

B3 —————: *Notizen zu "Liebelei".* In: Neue Blätter des Theaters in der Josefstadt. 1968/1969. [From "Nachlaß" section "Werke — Schicksal"].

B4 —————: *"Das arme Mädel" — Niederschrift des ersten Einfalls zu "Leibelei".* In: Neue Blätter des Theaters in der Josefstadt. 1968/1969.

B5   SCHNITZLER, ARTHUR: *Das Wort. Bühnenmanuskript.* Ed. Friedrich Schreyvogl. Frankfurt a.M.: S. Fischer Verlag, 1969. [Published in mimeographed form].

B6   SCHNITZLER, ARTHUR: *Das Haus Delorme. Eine Familienszene.* Ed. Reinhard Urbach. In: Ver Sacrum. Neue Hefte für Kunst und Literatur. 1970, 46-55.

B7   ––––: *Zug der Schatten.* Ed. Françoise Derré. Frankfurt a.M.: S. Fischer Verlag, 1970, 120 p.
Reviewed by:
B7.1 Bergel, Kurt. In: MAL, 6, iii/iv (1973), 202-208.
B7.2 Branscombe, Peter. In: Germanistik, 15, iii (1974), 728-729.
B7.3 Weber, Eugene. In: BA, 45, iii (1971), 513-514.

B8   SCHNITZLER, ARTHUR: *Aus Authur Schnitzlers Werkstatt. Unveröffentlichte Entwürfe und Szenen.* In: NZZ, Nr. 25, January 17, 1971.

B9   SCHNITZLER, ARTHUR: *Materialien zu "Das weite Land".* In: Programmheft des Theaters in der Josefstadt, Spielzeit 1972/73 (Premiere October 11, 1972). [Contains significant information on "Das weite Land"]

B10   SCHNITZLER, ARTHUR: *Materialien zu "Liebelei".* In: Programmheft des Wiener Burgtheaters. Gastspiel in Düsseldorf September 15, 1973. [Contains significant information on "Liebelei"].

B11   SCHNITZLER, ARTHUR: *Ritterlichkeit.* Fragment aus dem Nachlaß. Ed. Rena R. Schlein. Bonn: Bouvier Verlag, 1975, 112 p.
Reviewed by:
B11.1 g.a. [Gerty Aposton]. In: New York Staats-Zeitung und Herold. July 24/25, 1976.
B11.2 F.K. In: Wiener Zeitung, Nr. 134, June 11, 1976.
B11.3 Wagner, Renate: In: Neues Volksblatt, Nr. 223, September 24, 1976.

B12   SCHNITZLER, ARTHUR: *Wahrheit*. Fragment aus dem Nachlaß. Ed. Jeffrey B. Berlin. In: J.B.B. The Treatment of Truth in the Dramatic Work of Henrik Ibsen and Arthur Schnitzler. Ph.D. diss. State University of New York at Binghamton, 1976, pp. 214-217.

B13   — — — — —: *Daten zur Entstehung Schnitzlers "Im Spiel der Sommerlüfte"*. Ed. Reinhard Urbach. In: Programmheft des Theaters in der Josefstadt, Spielzeit 1976/77 (Premiere October 7, 1976), pp. 19-22.

B14   — — — — —: *Materialien zur Entstehungsgeschichte von Arthur Schnitzlers Tragikomödie "Das weite Land."* In: Programmheft Basler Theater. H. 9 (Premiere March 5, 1976). [Contains first publication of the first draft that led to "Das weite Land," the story "Frieberg," as well as additional material pertaining to the play.]

C. *Aphorisms, Essays, Sketches, Notes and Philosophical Writings*

1967

C1   SCHNITZLER, ARTHUR: *Gesammelte Werke: Aphorismen und Betrachtungen.* Ed. Robert O. Weiss. Frankfurt a.M.: S. Fischer Verlag, 1967, 516 p.
Reviewed by:
C1.1 Doppler, Alfred. In: Die Zeit im Buch (Wien), Nov./Dec., 1968.
C1.2 Farese, Giuseppe. In: Studi Germanici, 6, ii (1968), 155-168.
C1.3 Graf, Hansjörg. In: Wort und Wahrheit, 23, iv (1968), 378-379.
C1.4 Illing, Hans. In: MAL, 1, ii (1968), 43-44.
C1.5 Ivask, Ivar. In: BA, 42, iii (1968), 427-428.
C1.6 Kreuzer, Helmut. In: Germanistik, 9, iii (1968), 644-645.
C1.7 Offermanns, Ernst. In: Neue Deutsche Hefte, 15, i (1968), 216-220.
C1.8 Schmiele, Walter. In: Frankfurter Rundschau. March 1, 1968.
C1.9 Urbach, Reinhard. In: Neue Wege. Kulturschrift junger Menschen. Nr. 232, Jg. 23 (Dezember, 1968), 9-11.

1968

C2   SCHNITZLER, ARTHUR: *Jugend in Wien: Eine Autobiographie.* Ed. Heinrich Schnitzler and Therese Nickl. Wien: Fritz Molden Verlag, 1968, 384 p.
Reviewed by:
C2.1 Derré, Françoise. In: Germanistik, 10, ii (1969), 455.
C2.2 Fackert, Jürgen. In: Schweizer Monatshefte, 49, x (1970), 976-979.

C2.3 Foltin, Lore B. In: MAL, 3, iii (1970), 47.
C2.4 Heller, Francis H. In: Modern Drama, 13, i (1970), 101-103.
C2.5 Lederer, Herbert. In: GQ, 43, i (1970), 117-119.
C2.6 Politzer, Heinz. In: Christ und Welt, 22, ii (10.1.1969), 14.
C2.7 Weiss, Robert O. In: AGR, 35, v (1969), 22-23.

1969

C3   SCHNITZLER, ARTHUR: *Bestimmungen über meinen schriftlichen Nachlaß.* In: Gerhard Neumann and Jutta Müller, Der Nachlaß Arthur Schnitzlers. Munich: Wilhelm Fink Verlag, 1969, pp. 23-38.

C4   ––––: *Zu Thomas Manns 50. Geburtstag.* In: Thomas Mann im Urteil seiner Zeit. Dokumente 1891-1955. Ed. Klaus Schröder. Hamburg: Christian Wegner Verlag, 1969, pp. 125-126. [First in: Berliner Tageblatt, June 6 [7?], 1925].

1970

C5   SCHNITZLER, ARTHUR: *Grabrede für Otto Brahm.* In: NZZ, Nr. 425, Sept. 13, 1970. (Dated Nov. 30, 1912).

C6   ––––: *Notizen über Karl Kraus.* Ed. Reinhard Urbach. In: LuK, 49 (1970), 523-524.

1972

C7   SCHNITZLER, ARTHUR: *"Geist lebt vom Zuwenig der Worte." Unveröffentlichte literarische Notizen Arthur Schnitzlers.* Ed. Reinhard Urbach. In: NZZ, Nr. 362, August 6, 1972, 43. [Schnitzler's criticism of literary works by Hauptmann, Werfel, Kraus, etc.]

1973

C8   SCHNITZLER, ARTHUR: *Notizen zu Lektüre und Theaterbesuchen (1879-1927).* Ed. Reinhard Urbach. In: MAL, 6, iii/iv (1973), 7-39.

1975

C9   *Arthur Schnitzler: Hugo von Hofmannsthal. "Charakteristik aus den Tagebüchern."* Ed. Bernd Urban, in collaboration with Werner Volke. In: Hofmannsthal-Forschungen III. Freiburg im Breisgau: Hugo von Hofmannsthal Gesellschaft, 1975, 97 p.

1976

C10 SCHNITZLER, ARTHUR: *Über Psychoanalyse.* Ed. Reinhard Urbach. In: Protokolle, 2 (1976), 277-284. [Newly discovered notes by Schnitzler].

C11   ─────: *Diary Notations on Henrik Ibsen.* From the Nachlaß. Ed.
Jeffrey B. Berlin. In: J.B.B. The Treatment of Truth in the Dramatic
Work of Henrik Ibsen and Arthur Schnitzler. Ph.D. diss. State
University of New York at Binghamton, 1976, pp. 17-19.

C12   ─────: *Ibsen Plays Seen by Schnitzler: 1890-1931.* From the
Nachlaß. Ed. Jeffrey B. Berlin. In: J.B.B. The Treatment of Truth in
the Dramatic Work of Henrik Ibsen and Arthur Schnitzler. Ph.D.
diss. State University of New York at Binghamton, 1976, pp.
470-472.

C13   ─────: *Schnitzlers Nordlandreise: 1896.* From the Nachlaß. Ed.
Jeffrey B. Berlin. In: J.B.B. The Treatment of Truth in the Dramatic
Work of Henrik Ibsen and Arthur Schnitzler. Ph.D. diss. State
University of New York at Binghamton, 1976, pp. 41-42.

1977

C14   *Theodor Reik: Letters to Arthur Schnitzler.* Ed. Jeffrey B. Berlin.
In: The Psychoanalytic Review. (To appear May, 1978.) [Nineteen
newly discovered letters from Reik to Schnitzler, dated from 1912
to 1929. Letters plus commentary.]

C15   ARTHUR SCHNITZLER: *Gesammelte Werke, Bd. 6: Entworfenes
und Verworfenes. Aus dem Nachlaß.* Zusammengestellt und
eigeleitet von Reinhard Urbach. Frankfurt a.M.: S. Fischer Verlag,
1977.

C16   *The Letters of Arthur Schnitzler to Hermann Bahr.* Ed. Donald G.
Daviau. (To appear 1977/1978). Chapel Hill: The University of
North Carolina Press.

D. *Correspondence*

1965

D1   SCHNITZLER, ARTHUR: *Brief an Richard Charmatz.* In:
Programmheft zur Aufführung "Professor Bernhardi" am
Akademietheater Wien, 1965. Also in: Theater heute, 5, xii (1964),
32-33. [Letter of Jan. 4, 1913 that discusses "Professor
Bernhardi"].

1966

D2   SCHNITZLER, ARTHUR: *Letzter Brief an Hugo von Hofmannsthal.* In: Almanach. Das achtzigste Jahr. Frankfurt a.M.: S.
Fischer Verlag, 1966, p. 37. [Letter dated July 25, 1929; also
contains facsimile of letter].

D3   ─────: *Brief an Nathan Ausubel.* In: NZZ, Nr. 91/92, January 9,
1966, 4. [Letter of July 17, 1924].

D4 ─────: *Brief an Sylvia Beach.* In: NZZ, Nr. 92/1, January 9, 1966, 5. [Letter of Jan. 13, 1927].

D5 ─────: *Brief an Paul Block.* In: NZZ, Nr. 91/2, January 9, 1966, 4. [Letter of Jan. 27, 1915].

D6 ─────: *Brief an Tilla Durieux.* In: NZZ, Nr. 92/1, January 9, 1966, 5. [Letter of Feb. 21, 1921].

D7 ─────: *Brief an Stefan Grossmann.* In: NZZ, Nr. 91/2, January 9, 1966, 4. [Letter of Feb. 12, 1913].

D8 ─────: *Brief an Willy Hass.* In: NZZ, Nr. 92/1, January 9, 1966, 5. [Letter of Sept. 24, 1930].

D9 ─────: *Brief an Theodor Herzl.* In: NZZ, Nr. 91/2, January 9, 1966, 5. [Letter of Nov. 12, 1892].

D10 ─────: *Brief an Jakob Lipowitz.* In: NZZ, Nr. 92/1, January 9, 1966, 5. [Letter of May 23, 1925].

D11 ─────: *Brief an Heinrich Mann.* In: NZZ, Nr. 91/2, January 9, 1966, 4. [Letter of Oct. 3, 1917].

D12 *Korrespondenz zwischen Arthur Schnitzler und Peter Altenberg.* In: "Einleitung" to "Das Wort," by Arthur Schnitzler, ed. Kurt Bergel. Frankfurt a.M.: S. Fischer Verlag, 1966, pp. 7-11. Also in: Kurt Bergel, "Arthur Schnitzlers unveröffentlichte Tragikomödie 'Das Wort'," Studies in Arthur Schnitzler, ed. Herbert W. Reichert and Herman Salinger, Chapel Hill: University of North Carolina Press, 1963, p. 19, n. 12. [Cf. Reinhard Urbach, " 'Schwätzer sind Verbrecher.' Bermerkungen zu Schnitzlers Dramenfragment 'Das Wort'," LuK, 25 (1968), esp. pp. 292-293.]

1967

D13 SCHNITZLER, ARTHUR: *Briefe an Josef Körner.* Ed. Reinhard Urbach. In: LuK, 12 (1967), 79-87. [Letters of March 20, 1926, Jan. 19, 1931 and April 8, 1931].

D14 ─────: *Brief an Herrn Graetzer.* Ed. Reinhard Urbach. In: LuK, 12 (1967), 78. [Letter of May 3, 1910].

D15 ─────: *Brief an Irma Janiczek.* Ed. Reinhard Urbach. In: LuK, 13 (1967), 134. [Letter of Feb. 3, 1904. Listed as "Aus der Korrespondenz mit unbekannten Autoren;" now identified by Reinhard Urbach].

D16 ─────: *Brief an Marie Schmid.* Ed. Reinhard Urbach. In: LuK, 12 (1967), 87. [Letter of June 9, 1909. Listed as "Aus der Korrespondenz mit unbekannten Autoren;" now identified by Reinhard Urbach].

1968

D17 MUSIL, ROBERT: *Lettre à Arthur Schnitzler.* Ed. Marie-Louise Roth. In: EG, 23, iii (1968), 401.

[Letter of Dec. 3, 1921 which asks Schnitzler to publish in the "Prager Presse;" reprinted in: Robert Musil. Briefe nach Prag. Ed. Barbara Lopplová and Kurt Krolop. Reinbek bei Hamburg: Rowohlt Verlag, 1971, p. 101.]

D18   SCHNITZLER, ARTHUR: *Brief an Peter Altenberg.* In: Reinhard Urbach, " 'Schwätzer sind Verbrecher'. Bermerkungen zu Schnitzlers Dramenfragment 'Das Wort'," LuK, 25 (1968), 293. [Letter of Oct. 20, 1896].

D19   ––––––: *Brief an Graf Richard Nikolaus Coudenhove-Kalergi.* In: "Briefe zur Politik." Ed. Reinhard Urbach, Forum, 15 (1968). [Letter of Dec. 7, 1929].

D20   ––––––: *Brief an Alfred H. Fried.* In: "Briefe zur Politik." Ed. Reinhard Urbach, Forum, 15 (1968), 679. [Letter of March 19, 1919].

D21   ––––––: *Brief an Dr. Gelber.* In: "Briefe zur Politik." Ed. Reinhard Urbach, Forum, 15 (1968), 679. [Letter of Dec. 22, 1915].

D22   ––––––: *Brief an Isaac Levine.* In: "Briefe zur Politik." Ed. Reinhard Urbach, Forum, 15 (1968), 680. [Letter of April 14, 1926].

D23   ––––––: *Briefe an Elisabeth Steinrück.* In: "Briefe zur Politik." Ed. Reinhard Urbach, Forum, 15 (1968), 677-678. [Letters of Dec. 22 and 26, 1914].

1969

D24   WALTER, BRUNO: *Brief an Arthur Schnitzler.* In: Bruno Walter. Briefe 1894-1962. Ed. Lotte Walter Lindt. Frankfurt a.M.: S. Fischer Verlag, 1969, pp. 98-99. [Letter of June 6, 1908].

D25   ––––––: *Brief an Olga Schnitzler.* In: Bruno Walter. Briefe 1894-1962 Ed. Lotte Walter Lindt. Frankfurt a.M.: S. Fischer Verlag, 1969, pp. 100-101. [Letter of July 31, 1908].

1970

D26   FISCHER, S.: *Briefe an Arthur Schnitzler.* In: Peter de Mendelssohn, S. Fischer und sein Verlag, Frankfurt a.M.: S. Fischer Verlag, 1970. [Contains previously unpublished letters].

D27   KRAUS, KARL: *Briefe an Arthur Schnitzler.* In: "Karl Kraus und Arthur Schnitzler: Eine Dokumentation." Ed. Reinhard Urbach, LuK, 49 (1970), 513-529.

D28   SCHNITZLER, ARTHUR: *Brief an Max Reinhardt.* In: NZZ, Nr. 425, September 13, 1970. [Letter of Dec. 24, 1909; now in "Der Briefwechsel Arthur Schnitzlers mit Max Reinhardt und dessen Mitarbeitern," ed. Renate Wagner. Salzburg: Otto Müller Verlag, 1971].

D29 ─────: *Liebe, die starb vor der Zeit. Arthur Schnitzler – Olga Waissnix. Ein Briefwechsel.* Ed. Heinrich Schnitzler and Therese Nickl. Wien: Verlag Fritz Molden, 1970, 422 p.
Reviewed by:
D29.1 Kimpel, Dieter. In: Germanistik, 13, iv (1972), 792.
D29.2 Nehring, Wolfgang. In: GQ, 45, i (1972), 188-191.
D29.3 Swales, Martin. In: BA, 45, iv (1971), 693.

1971

D30 MANN, HEINRICH: *Briefe an Arthur Schnitzler.* In: Heinrich Mann 1871-1950. Werk und Leben in Dokumenten und Bildern. Ed. Deutsche Akademie der Künste zu Berlin. Berlin and Weimar: Aufbau-Verlag, 1971, pp. 177 and 197-198. [Letters of May 11, 1912 and Oct. 4, 1923].

D31 MANN, THOMAS: *To Arthur Schnitzler.* In: Letters of Thomas Mann 1899-1955. Tr. Richard and Clara Winston. New York: Alfred A. Knopf, 1971, pp. 118-119. [Letter of Sept. 4, 1922; in English translation. First in: Thomas Mann. Briefe 1889-1936. Ed. Erika Mann. Frankfurt a.M.: S. Fischer Verlag, 1962, pp. 199-200. This edition also contains [p. 102] T. M.'s letter of May 22, 1913 to Schnitzler, which is not recorded in the Allen bibliography].

D32 SCHNITZLER, ARTHUR: *Briefe an Heinrich Mann.* In: Heinrich Mann 1871-1950. Werk und Leben in Dokumenten und Bildern. Ed. Deutsche Akademie der Künste zu Berlin. Berlin and Weimar: Aufbau-Verlag, 1971, pp. 142 and 206. [Letters of Jan. 3, 1919 (previously published in Die Neue Rundschau, 68, 1 (1957), 98) and Feb. 9, 1922].

D33 : *Brief an Marie Herzfeld.* Ed. Reinhard Urbach. In: Hofmannsthal Blätter, H. 6 (1971), 442. [Letter of Jan. 29, 1908].

D34 ─────: *Der Briefwechsel Arthur Schnitzlers mit Max Reinhardt und dessen Mitarbeitern.* Ed. Renate Wagner. Salzburg: Otto Müller Verlag, 1971, 145 p.
Reviewed by:
D34.1 haj [Hansres Jacobi]. In: Neue Zürcher Zeitung, Nr. 412 (Sept. 5, 1971).
D34.2 Kluge, Gerhard. In: Germanistik, 13, i (1972), 195-196.
D34.3 Roelofs, Hans. In: Het Duitse Boek (the Netherlands), 3 (1972), 94-95.
D34.4 Swales, Martin. In: BA, 46, ii (1972), 299-300.

D35 *Arthur Schnitzler – Franz Nabl. Briefwechsel.* Ed. Reinhard Urbach. In: Studium Generale, 24 (1971), 1256-1270.

1972

D36   SCHNITZLER, ARTHUR: *Brief an Heinrich Schnitzler*. Ed. Reinhard Urbach. In: Neue Blätter des Theaters in der Josefstadt, 1972. [Letter dated Sept. 5, 1931 concerning his son's first Viennese production].

D37   ————: *The Correspondence of Arthur Schnitzler and Raoul Auernheimer with Raoul Auernheimer's Aphorisms*. Ed. Donald G. Daviau and Jorun B. Johns. Chapel Hill: University of North Carolina Press, 1972, 160 p.
Reviewed by:
D37.1 Aspetsberger, Friedbert. In: Germanistik, 14, iv (1973), 899-900.
D37.2 Boelcskevy, Andrew. In: BA, 48, i (1974), 143-144.
D37.3 Derré, Françoise. In: EG, 28, iv (1973), 544-545.
D37.4 Schlein, Rena R. In: Monatshefte, 66, i (1974), 79-80.
D37.5 Swales, Martin. In: GL&L, 28, ii (1975), 178-179.
D37.6 Zohn, Harry. In: MAL, 6, i/ii (1973), 204-209.

1973

D38   FISCHER, HEDWIG: *Brief an Arthur Schnitzler*. In: Almanach. Das siebenundachtzigste Jahr. Frankfurt a.M.: S. Fischer Verlag, 1973, pp. 147-148. [Letter of July 19, 1929 concerning death of Hugo von Hofmannsthal].

1974

D39   SCHNITZLER, ARTHUR: *Briefe zum Reigen*. Ed. Reinhard Urbach. In: Ver Sacrum. Neue Hefte für Kunst und Literatur. 1974. [Four letters to Dora Michaelis; one to Prof. Richter].

D40   *Arthur Schnitzler – Thomas Mann: Briefe*. Ed. Hertha Krotkoff. In: MAL, 7, i/ii (1974), 1-33.

1975

D41   *Der Briefwechsel Arthur Schnitzler – Otto Brahm*. Vollständige Ausgabe. Ed. Oskar Seidlin. 2nd edition. Tübingen: Max Niemeyer Verlag, 1975, 362 p.
Reviewed by:
D41.1 Kauf, Robert. In: BA, 50, iv (1976), 871.

D42   *Dilly. Adele Sandrock und Arthur Schnitzler. Geschichte einer Liebe in Briefen, Bildern und Dokumenten*. Ed. Renate Wagner. Wien: Amalthea Verlag, 1975, 400 p.
Reviewed by:
D42.1 Lahann, Birgit. In: Die Welt. Nr. 296, Dec. 20, 1975.

D43   *Arthur Schnitzler – Richard Schaukal Briefwechsel (1900-1902).* Ed. Reinhard Urbach. In: MAL, 8, iii/iv (1975), 15-42.

D44   *Vier unveröffentliche Briefe Arthur Schnitzlers an den Psychoanalytiker Theodor Reik.* Ed. Bernd Urban. In: Programm der Veranstaltungsreihe Wege und Gestalten, Frühjahr 1975. Also in: MAL, 8, iii/iv (1975), 236-247.

E. *Poetry*

1968

E1   SCHNITZLER, ARTHUR: *Ballade von den drei Brüdern.* Ed. Reinhard Urbach. In: Forum, 15 (1968), 676.

1970

E2   SCHNITZLER, ARTHUR: *Frühe Gedichte.* Ed. Herbert Lederer. Berlin: Propyläen Verlag, 1970, 86 p.
Reviewed by:
E.2.1 Angress, Ruth K. In: Monatshefte, 63, iii (1971), 293-294.
E2.2 Nehring, Wolfgang. In: GQ, 44, iv (1971), 607-608

F. *Music*

1968

F1   SCHNITZLER, ARTHUR: *Liebelei Walzer.* Wien: Josef Hochmuth Musikverlag, 1968, 3 p.

G. *Translations*

1967

G1   SCHNITZLER, ARTHUR: *The Game of Love (Liebelei).* Tr. Carl Mueller. In: Masterpieces of the Modern Central European Theatre, ed. Robert W. Corrigan. New York: Collier, 1967, pp. 41-93.

G2   –––––: *La Ronde (Reigen).* Tr. Carl Mueller. In: Masterpieces of the Modern Central European Theatre, ed. Robert W. Corrigan, New York: Collier, 1967, pp. 95-159. [This translation first in: The Modern Theatre, ed. Robert W. Corrigan. New York: The Macmillan Comapny, 1964].

G3   –––––: *From Book of Aphorisms and Considerations.* Tr. Carl Mueller. In: Masterpieces of the Modern Central European Theatre, ed. Robert W. Corrigan. New York: Collier, 1967, pp. 35-39. [These translations first in: The Modern Theatre, ed. Robert W. Corrigan. New York: The Macmillan Company, 1964].

G4   —————: *Anatol.* Tr. Paolo Chiarini. Rome: Edizioni dell'Ateneo, 1967, 363 p. [Dual text: German and Italian].
Reviewed by:
G4.1 David, Sante. In: Germanistik, 10, ii (1969), 454.

1969

G5   SCHNITZLER, ARTHUR: *Fräulein Else.* Tr. Harry Steinhauer. In: H. S., Ten German Novellas. New York: Doubleday & Company, Inc., 1969, pp. 471-529.

1970

G6   SCHNITZLER, ARTHUR: *My Youth in Vienna.* Tr. Catherine Hutter. New York: Holt, Rinehart and Winston, Inc., 1970, 304 p.
Reviewed by:
G6.1 Heller, Erich. In: Saturday Review, Jan. 16, 1971, 29-30 & 58.

G7   —————: *Redogonda's Diary.* Tr. Eric Sutton. In: Great Love Stories of All Ages, ed. Robert Lynd. New York: Spring Books, 1970, pp. 527-532. [Reprint of 1932 edition; London: George G. Harrap & Co., Ltd.].

1971

G8   SCHNITZLER, ARTHUR: *Beatrice.* Tr. Agnes Jacques. New York: AMS Press, Inc., 1971, 173 p. [Reprint of 1926 edition; New York: Simon & Schuster].

G9   —————: *Casanova's Homecoming.* Tr. Eden and Cedar Paul. New York: AMS Press, Inc., 1971, 187 p. [Reprint of 1930 edition; New York: Simon & Schuster].

G10   —————: *Daybreak.* Tr. William A. Drake. New York: AMS Press, Inc., 1971, 204 p. [Reprint of 1927 edition; New York: Simon & Schuster].

G11   —————: *Dr. Graesler.* Tr. E. C. Slade. New York: AMS Press, Inc., 1971, 176 p. [Reprint of 1930 edition; New York: Simon & Schuster].

G12   —————: *Fräulein Else.* Tr. Robert A. Simon. New York: AMS Press, 1971, 145 p. [Reprint of 1925 edition; New York: Simon & Schuster].

G13   —————: *Flight into Darkness.* Tr. William A. Drake. New York AMS Press, 1971, 154 p. [Reprint of 1931 edition; New York: Simon & Schuster].

G14   —————: *None But the Brave.* Tr. Richard L. Simon. New York: AMS Press, Inc., 1971, 74 p. [Reprint of 1926 edition; New York: Simon & Schuster].

G15 ––––––: *Professor Bernhardi.* Tr. Hetty Landstone. New York: AMS Press, Inc., 1971, 160 p. [Reprint of 1928 edition; New York: Simon & Schuster].

G16 ––––––: *Rhapsody; A Dream Novel.* Tr. Otto P. Schinnerer. New York: AMS Press, Inc., 1971, 192 p. [Reprint of 1927 edition; Simon & Schuster].

G17 ––––––: *Theresa, The Chronicle of a Woman's Life.* Tr. William A. Drake. New York: AMS Press, Inc. 1971, 460 p. [Reprint of 1928 edition; New York: Simon & Schuster].

G18 ––––––: *Novelle.* Tr. Giuseppe Farese. Rome: Edizioni dell'Ateneo, 1971, 565 p. [Italian translations of "Sterben," "Blumen," "Die Frau des Weisen," "Die Toten schweigen," "Leutnant Gustl," "Der blinde Geromino und sein Bruder," "Der Fremde," "Das Schicksal des Freiherrn von Leisenbohg," "Die Hirtenflöte," "Fräulein Else," "Traumnovelle," and "Flucht in die Finsternis"].
Reviewed by:
G18.1 Aspetsberger, Friedbert. In: Germanistik, 14, ii (1973), 491.

1972

G19 SCHNITZLER, ARTHUR: *The Mind in Words and Actions. Preliminary Remarks Concerning Two Diagrams.* Tr. Robert O. Weiss. New York: Frederick Ungar, 1972, 59 p.
Reviewed by:
G19.1 Carter, David R. In: Germanistik, 14, iii (1973), 735.

G19.2 Lawson, Richard H. In: MAL, 5, i/ii (1972), 149-151.
G19.3 Swales, Martin. In: BA, 47, ii (1973), 359.

G20 ––––––: *Some Day Peace Will Return Notes on War and Peace.* Tr. Robert O. Weiss. New York: Frederick Ungar, 1972, 102 p.
Reviewed by:
G20.1 Lawson, Richard H. In: MAL, 5, i/ii (1972), 151-154.
G20.2 Swales, Martin. In: BA, 47, ii (1973), 359.

1973

G21 SCHNITZLER, ARTHUR: *Round Dance (Reigen).* Tr. Eric Bentley. In: Themes of Drama. An Anthology. Ed. George E. Wellwarth. New York: Thomas Y. Crowell Company, 1973, pp. 333-365. [Reprint of previous translation by E.B.].

1974

G22 SCHNITZLER, ARTHUR: *Vienna 1900. Games with Love and Death.* New York: Penguin Books Inc., 1974, 365 p. [English translations of "Frau Beate und ihr Sohn," "Der Mörder," "Dr. Graesler. Badearzt" and "Frau Bertha Garlan." Reprint of earlier translations].

G23 ———: *Little Novels.* Tr. Eric Sutton. New York: AMS Press, Inc. 1974, 279 p. [Reprint of 1929 edition; New York: Simon & Schuster. English translations of "Das Schicksal des Freiherrn von Leisenbohg," "Die Fremde," "Die griechische Tänzerin," "Die Weissagung," "Der blinde Geronimo und sein Bruder," "Andreas Thameyers letzter Brief," "Das Tagebuch der Redegonda," "Der tote Gabriel," "Der Mörder," and "Der Tod des Junggesellen"].

G24 ———: *Viennese Novelettes.* New York: AMS Press, Inc., 1974, 433 p. [Reprint of 1931 edition; New York: Simon & Schuster. Contents: introduction by Otto P. Schinnerer; English translations of "Spiel im Morgengrauen," "Fräulein Else," "Traumnovelle," "Frau Beate und ihr Sohn," and "Leutnant Gustl"].

1975

G25 SCHNITZLER, ARTHUR: *Il ritorno di Casanova.* Traduzione e nota a cura di Giuseppe Farese. Milano: Adelphi Edizioni, 1975, 149 p. [Italian translation of "Casanovas Heimfahrt" with a postscript by G. F.].
Reviewed by:
G25.1 Chiusano, Italo A. In: Il Popolo (Roma). Sept. 3, 1975.
G25.2 dell'Arco, Mario. In: Giornale di Brescia (Brescia). Aug. 13, 1975.
G25.3 Faggi, Vico. In: Giornale di Brescia (Brescia). July 17, 1975.
G25.4 Gibellini, Pietro. In: Nuovo Brescia Oggi (Brescia). Aug. 31, 1975.
G25.5 Giuliani, Alfredo. In: Il Messaggero (Roma). Oct. 16, 1975.
G25.6 Guglielmi, Edoardo. In: Avvenire (Milano). Oct. 4, 1975.
G25.7 Manacorda, Giorgio. In: La Stampa (Torino). Aug. 8, 1975.
G25.8 Masini, Ferruccio. In: L'Unita (Roma-Milano). Dec. 5, 1975.
G25.9 Restagno, Enzo. In: Il Resto del Carlino (Bologna). Oct. 7, 1975.
G25.10 Saracino, Doriano. In: Momento Sera (Roma). Aug. 13, 1975.
G25.11 Sibilio, Angelo. In: Gazzetta di Parma (Parma). Aug. 7, 1975.
G25.12 Zampa, Giorgio. In: Il Giornale (Milano). Aug. 27, 1975.

G26 ———: *"Girotondo"* ["Reigen"] Traduzione di Paolo Chiarini. Torino: Giulio Einaudi editores, 1975, 74 p.

G27 STAMON, PEGGY: *New Translations of Three Arthur Schnitzler Stories.* 132 p. M.A. Thesis, San Diego State University. [English translations of "Der blinde Geronimo und sein Bruder," "Die Toten schweigen," and "Der Tod des Junggesellen." Includes introduction and critical comments].

H. *Secondary Literature*

1965

H1 ALEXANDER, THEODOR W.: *The Author's Debt to the Physician: Aphonia in the Works of Arthur Schnitzler.* In: JIASRA, 4, iv (1965), 4-15.

H2 ASPETSBERGER, FRIEDBERT: *Der Prozess gegen die Berliner Aufführung des 'Reigen', 1922.* In: Akzente, 12 (1965), 211-230.

H3 BAUMANN, GERHART: *Arthur Schnitzler. Die Welt von Gestern eines Dichters von Morgen.* Frankfurt a.M.: Athenäum, 43 p.
Reviewed by:
H3.1 DeBoer, R. In: Neophilologus, 51, ii (1967), 207-208.
H3.2 Derré, Françoise. In: EG, 22 (1967), 639.
H3.3 Illing, Hans. In: JIASRA, 6, ii (1967), 39-40.
H3.4 Jacobs, M. In: MLR, 62, iv (1967), 759-760.
H3.5 Müller, Joachim. In: Germanistik, 8, ii (1967), 408.
H3.6 Seidler, Ingo. In: Colloquia Germinica (1969), 354-355.
H3.7 Weiss, Robert O. In: MP, 65, ii (1967), 180-181.
H3.8 Wightmann, P. H. In: GL&L, 21, ii (1968), 168-169,

H4 HUTSCHNEIDER, JOSEF: *Arthur Schnitzler als Aphoristiker. Bermerkungen zu seinem "Buch der Sprüche und Bedenken".* In: JIASRA, 4, ii (1965), 4-19.

H5 JÄGER, MANFRED: *Schnitzlers "Leutnant Gustl".* In: WW, 15, v (1965), 308-316.

H6 *Kindlers Literatur Lexikon* Wiss. Vorbereitung: W. v. Einsiedel. Zürich: Kindler Verlag, 1965ff. [Contains brief analysis, plot outline and significant information for selected works of Schnitzler. "Anatol:" vol. 1, pp. 617-618 with a photo of the cover design for the 1895 edition on p. 768; "Fräulein Else:" vol. III, pp. 195-197; "Der grüne Kakadu:" vol. III, pp. 1233-1234; "Komtesse Mizzi:" vol. IV, pp. 649-650; "Liebelei:" vol. IV, pp. 1388-1390; "Leutnant Gustl:" vol. IV, pp. 1407-1409; "Professor Bernhardi:" vol. V, pp. 2637-2638; "Reigen:" vol. VI, pp. 94-97; "Spiel im Morgengrauen:" vol. VI, pp. 1823-1824; "Therese:" vol. VI, pp. 2595-2596; "Traumnovelle:" vol. VI, pp. 2971-2973; "Der Weg ins Freie:" vol. VII, pp. 1004-1006; "Das weite Land:" vol. VII, pp. 1030-1031].

H7 LEDERER, HERBERT: *Arthur Schnitzler's Influence on Modern Drama.* In: JIASRA, 4, i (1965), 16-17.

H8 *Literatur vor Gericht. Von "Les Fleurs du Mal" bis "Notre-Dame-des Fleurs".* In: Akzente 12 (1965), 210-251. [Pp. 211-230: discusses the proceedings of the Berlin production of "Reigen" in 1922].

H9   LoCICERO, DONALD: *Arthur Schnitzler and Eugene O'Neill: Masks, Pipedreams, and Reality.* In: JIASRA, 4, iii (1965), 27-42.

H10   LoCICERO, VINCENT: *Schnitzler, O'Neill, and Reality.* In: JIASRA, 4, iii (1965), 4-26.

H11   ————: *The "persona" in the works of Schnitzler and O'Neill.* In: JIASRA, 4, i (1965), 20-21

H12   ————: Rev. of Arthur Schnitzler's *Anatol,* ed. with a critical commentary by Ernst L. Offermanns. Berlin: Walter de Gruyter & Co., 1964, 202 p. in: JIASRA, 4, i (1965), 27.

H13   MARCUSE, LUDWIG: *Obscene. The History of an Indignation.* Tr. Karen Gershon. London: Macgibbon & Kee, 1965. ("Reigen:" pp. 167-214).

H14   MELCHINGER, SIEGFRIED: *Das Material der Stückeschreiber. Zum Briefwechsel zwischen Hofmannsthal und Schnitzlers.* In: Theater heute, 6, ii (1965), 40-41.

H15   MUSIL, ROBERT: *Theater. Kritisches und Theoretisches.* Ed. Marie-Louise Roth. Hamburg: Rowohlt Verlag, 1965. [Pp. 177-180 discusses Schnitzler].

H16   PICKERODT, GERHART: *Dichter-Briefwechsel. Anläßlich der Herausgabe des Briefwechsels Hofmannsthal-Schnitzler.* In: Du-Atlantis, 25 (1965), 473-474.

H17   REICHERT, HERBERT: *Schnitzlers egoistische Künstlergestalten.* In: JIASRA, 4, ii (1965), 20-27.

H18   REY, WILLIAM H.: *Arthur Schnitzler.* In: Deutsche Dichter der Moderne: Ihr Leben und Werk, ed. Benno von Wiese. Berlin: Erich Schmidt Verlag, 1965, pp. 237-257. [New edition published, 1975, contains up-to-date bibliography.]

H19   ROMANN, H. L.: *Arthur Schnitzlers Schauspiel "Liebelei".* In: Die Volksbühne, 16, vi (1965), 104-106.

H20   SALINGER, HERMAN: *Arthur Schnitzler's Influence as an Historian of Contemporary Society.* In: JIASRA, 4, i (1965), 17-19.

H21   SCHÄBLE, GÜNTHER: *Wie spielt man Schnitzlers Stücke?* In: Theater heute, 6, iv (1965), 35-36.

H22   SCHREYVOGL, FRIEDRICH: *Das Burgtheater.* Wien: F. Speidel-Verlag, 1965, 226 p. [Several references to Schnitzler].

H23   WEIGEL, HANS: *Die große Vergeblichkeit. Zum hundersten Geburtstag Arthur Schnitzlers.* In: H. W., Das tausendjährige Kind. Wien: Verlag Kremayr & Scheriau, 1965, pp. 152-171. [First in: NDH, 88 (1962), 25-43].

H24   ————: *Vorwort.* In: Arthur Schnitzler. Spiel im Morgengrauen und andere Erzählungen, ed. Hans Weigel. Zürich: Diogenes Verlag, 1965, pp. 7-14.

H25   ZAK, EDUARD and RUDOLF WALBINER: *Nachwort.* In: Arthur Schnitzler, "Erzählungen," ed. E. Z. and Christa Gähler. Berlin and Weimar: Aufbau-Verlag, 1965, pp. 380-391.

H26   ALLEN, RICHARD H.: *Schnitzler and his Early Critics*. In: JIASRA, 5, iii (1966), 17-21.

H27   —————: *An Annotated Arthur Schnitzler Bibliography. Editions and Criticism in German, French, and English 1879-1965.* Chapel Hill: University of North Carolina Press, 1966, 150 p.
Reviewed by:
H27.1 Berlin, Jeffrey. In: MAL, 3, iv (1970), 68.
H27.2 DeBoer, R. In: Neophilologus, 52, ii (1968), 221-222.
H27.3 Derré, Françoise. In: EG, 22, iv (1967), 639.
H27.4 Hannum, Hunter G. In: GQ, 41, iii (1968), 464-466.
H27.5 Jonas, Klaus W. In: JIASRA, 6, iv (1967), 45-47.
H27.6 Kuxdorf, Manfred. In: Seminar, 3, ii (1967), 160-161.
H27.7 LoCicero, Donald. In: MLN, 83, v (1968), 795-796.
H27.8 Rey, William H. In: JEGP, 66, iv (1967), 655-656.
H27.9 Urbach, Reinhard. In: LuK, 15, (1967), 324-328.
H27.10 Wagner, Renate. In: MuK, 16, iii/iv (1970), 329-331.

H28   ASPETSBERGER, FRIEDBERT: *"Drei Akte in einem".* *Zum Formtyp von Schnitzlers Drama*. In: ZDP, 85, ii (1966), 285-308.

H29   BERGEL, KURT: *Einleitung.* In: Arthur Schnitzler, "Das Wort", ed. Kurt Bergel. Frankfurt a.M.: S. Fischer Verlag, pp. 5-27.

H30   BLAUHUT, ROBERT: *Österreichische Novellistik des 20. Jahrhunderts.* Wien: Wilhelm Braumüller, 1966. [Pp. 22-28 discuss Schnitzler].

H31   BLÖCKER, GÜNTER: *Hugo von Hofmannsthal/Arthur Schnitzler Breifwechsel.* In: G. B., Literatur als Teilhabe. Kritische Orientierungen zur literarischen Gegenwart. Berlin: Argon Verlag, 1966, pp. 287-292.

H32   BLUME, BERNHARD: *Arthur Schnitzler.* In: B. B., Aufsätze aus dem Stuttgarter Neuen Tagblatt und der Stuttgarter Zeitung 1933-1966, pp. 23-26. Privately printed by the Stuttgarter Zeitung, 1966 on the occasion of B. B.'s 65th birthday. [Valuable overall evaluation; first appeared as "Bild einer verfallenden Welt. Zum 25. Todestag Arthur Schnitzlers," in: Stuttgarter Zeitung, 20. Oktober, 1956].

H33   BORTENSCHLAGER, WILHELM: *Deutsche Dichtung im 20. Jahrhundert.* Zürich: Verlagsbuchhandlung Leitner & Co., 1966. [Pp. 29-31: brief summaries of selected narrative and dramatic works of Schnitzler].

H34   DAVIAU, DONALD G.: *The Friendship of Hermann Bahr and Arthur Schnitzler.* In: JIASRA, 5, i (1966), 4-36.

H35   DERRÉ, FRANÇOISE: *L'oeuvre d'Arthur Schnitzler. Imagerie veinnoise et problèmes humains.* Paris: Marcel Didier, 1966, 519 p.

Reviewed by:

H35.1 Lederer, Herbert. In: JEGP, 67, i (1968), 130-133.

H35.2 Müller, Joachim. In: Germanistik, 9, i (1968), 179-180.

H35.3 Rey, William H. In: MAL, 1, ii (1968), 31-39.

H35.4 Roschitz, Karlheinz. In: LuK, 19 (1967), 563-565.

H35.5 Swales, Martin. In: MLR, 63, iii (1968), 759-761.

H36 ─────: *Une recontre singulière: J. Giraudoux et Arthur Schnitzler.* In: EG, 21, i (1966), 17-32.

H37 ─────: Rev. of Arthur Schnitzler's *Anatol,* ed. with a critical commentary by Ernst L. Offermanns. Berlin: Walter de Gruyter & Co., 1964, 202 p. In: EG, 21, iii (1966), 463.

H38 EWING, BLAIR: *The politics of Nihilism: Schnitzler's "Last Man".* In: JIASRA, 5, iii (1966), 4-16.

H39 FRIEDRICHSMEYER, ERHARD: *Zum "Augenblick" bei Schnitzler.* In: GRM, 16, i (1966), 52-64.

H40 FRITZ, WALTER: *Arthur Schnitzler und der Film.* In: JIASRA, 5, iv (1966), 11-52.

H41 GRANEEK, MYRA M.: *Arthur Schnitzler (1862-1931). A Revaluation.* In: Australasian Universities Language and Literature Association, 10 (1966), 284-294.

H42 KERNER, DIETER: *Der Arzt-Dichter Arthur Schnitzler 1862-1931.* In: Deutsches medizinisches Journal, 17, xviii (1966), 538-543.

H43 LEDERER, HERBERT: *Arthur Schnitzlers Autobiographie: Spiegel des Ichs und Spiegel der Welt.* In: JIASRA, 5, iv (1966), 4-10.

H44 MAGRIS, CLAUDIO: *Arthur Schnitzler.* In: C.M., Der habsburgische Mythos in der österreichischen Literatur. Salzburg: Otto Müller Verlag, 1966, pp. 202-214.

H45 PERL, WALTER: *Schnitzler, Hofmannsthal und Andrian in Jung Wien.* In: JIASRA, 5, iii (1966), 22-26.

H46 ─────: *Arthur Schnitzler und der junge Hofmannsthal.* In: Philobiblon, 10, iii (1966), 187-196.

H47 REICHERT, HERBERT: *Schnitzler and "Jung Wien."* In: JIASRA, 5, iii (1966), 27-32.

H48 REY, WILLIAM H.: *Die geistige Welt Arthur Schnitzlers.* In: WW, 16, iii (1966), 180-194.

H49 ─────: *"Arthur Schnitzler und Ich": Das Vermächtnis der Clara Katharina Pollaczek.* In: GR, 41, ii (1966), 120-135

H50 ROMANN, H.L.: *Arthur Schnitzlers "Der einsame Weg".* In: Die Volksbühne Blätter für Kunst und Volkskultur, 17, iii (1966), 56-58.

H51 STERN, J. P.: *Introduction.* In: Arthur Schnitzler, "Liebelei", "Leutnant Gustl", "Die letzten Masken", ed. J. P. Stern. Cambridge: The University Press, 1966, pp. 1-44. [Brief analysis of the three works].

Reviewed by:

H51.1 Hannum, Hunter G. In: GQ, 41, ii (1968), 271-272.

H52 STICCA, SANDRO: *The drama of being and seeming in Schnitzler's "Anatol" and Pirandello's "Cosi è se vi pare".* In: JIASRA, 5, ii (1966), 4-28.

H53 STOUT, HARRY: Rev. of *Studies in Arthur Schnitzler*, ed. Herbert W. Reichert and Herman Salinger. Chapel Hill: University of North Carolina Press, 1963, 116 p. In: MLN, 81, ii (1966), 254.

H54 TORBERG, FRIEDRICH: *Schnitzler*. In: F. T., *Das fünfte Rad am Thespiskarren.* Wien: Georg Müller Verlag, 1966, pp. 218-231. [Discusses Schnitzler's "Liebelei", "Komtesse Mizzi", "Der grüne Kakadu", "Das weite Land", "Anatol", "Professor Bernhardi", and "Komödie der Verführung"].

1967

H55 ADEL, KURT: *Arthur Schnitzler*. In: K. A., Geist und Wirklichkeit. Vom Werden der österreichischen Dichtung. Wien: Österreichische Verlagsanstalt, 1967, pp. 224-225.

H56 ALEXANDER, THEODOR W.: *Schnitzler and the inner monologue. A study in technique.* In: JIASRA, 6, ii (1967), 4-40.

H57 ALLEN, RICHARD: *Schnitzler's "Der Weg ins Freie": Structure or Structures?* In: JIASRA, 6, iii (1967), 4-17.

H58 BEHARRIELL, FREDERICK J.: *Schnitzler: Freuds Doppelgänger.* In: LuK, 19 (1967), 546-555. [First in: Journal of the American Psychological Association, 10, ix (1962), 722-730, in English].

H59 ─────: *Schnitzler's Vienna, 1966.* In: JIASRA, 6, i (1967), 4-13.

H60 CHIARINI, PAOLO: *Introduzione.* In: Arthur Schnitzler, "Anatol", ed. Paolo Chiarini. Rome. Edizioni dell'Ateneo, 1967, pp. VII-L.

H61 DUHAMEL, ROLAND: *Enkele beschwouwingen over Arthur Schnitzlers Aforismen.* In: RLV, 33, iii (1967), 289-296.

H62 GRAF, HANSJÖRG: *Nuancen der Freundschaft. Zu Hofmannsthals Korrespondenz mit Schnitzler und Karl von Bebenburg.* In: Wort und Wahrheit, 22, v (1967), 383-386.

H63 HANNUM, HUNTER G.: *"Merely Players": The Theatrical Worlds of Arthur Schnitzler and Jean Genet.* In: Festschrift fur Bernhard Blume, ed. Egon Schwarz, Hunter G. Hannum and Edgar Lohner. Göttingen: Vandenhoeck & Ruprecht, 1967, pp. 367-384.

H64 HERMAND, JOST: Rev. of Arthur Schnitzler's *Anatol*, ed. with a critical commentary by Ernst L. Offermanns. Berlin: Walter de Gruyter & Co., 1964, 202 p. In: Monatshefte, 59, iii (1967), 284-285.

H65 HORWATH, PETER: *Arthur Schnitzlers "Professor Bernhardi": Eine Studie über Person und Tendenz.* In: LuK, 12 (1967), 88-104.

H66 ─────: *Arthur Schnitzlers "Professor Bernhardi": Eine Studie über Person und Tendenz (II. Teil und Schluß).* In: LuK, 13, (1967), 183-193.

H67   IGGERS, WILMA A.: *Karl Kraus. A Viennese Critic of the Twentieth Century.* The Hague: Martinus Nijhoff, 1967, 248 p. [Pp. 74-75: Kraus on Schnitzler].

H68   JHERING, HERBERT: *"Reigen".* In: H. J., Von Reinhardt bis Brecht. Eine Auswahl der Theaterkritiken 1909-1932, ed. Rolf Badenhausen. Reinbek bei Hamburg: Rowohlt Verlag, 1967, pp. 77-79.

H69   KAFKA, FRANZ: *Briefe an Felice.* Ed. Erich Heller and Jürgen Born. Frankfurt a.M.: S. Fischer Verlag, 1967. [Pp. 299 (letter of Feb. 14 to 15, 1913) and 306 (letter of Feb. 18 to 19, 1913): express Kafka's extreme dislike of Schnitzler's works. English translation, Schocken Books, 1973.]

H70   KANN, ROBERT A.: *Arthur Schnitzler: Reflections on the Evolution of his Image.* In: Wisconsin Studies in Contemporary Literature, 8, iv (1967), 548-555.

H71   KERNER, DIETER: *Arzt — Dichter. Lebensbilder aus 5 Jahrhunderten. Eine Auswahl.* Stuttgart: Schattauer Verlag, 1967, esp. pp. 117-132.

H72   KLABES, GÜNTER: *Arthur Schnitzler: "Der Tod des Junggesellen" (Stilanalyse).* In: JIASRA, 6, iii (1967), 31-39.

H73   KUXDORF, MANFRED: *Arthur Schnitzler und der Zufall.* In: JIASRA, 6, iv (1967), 4-12.

H74   LEDERER, HERBERT: *Arthur Schnitzler als Lyriker.* In: Festschrift für Werner Neuse fides anlässlich des vierzigjährigen Bestehens der Deutschen Sommerschule am Middelbury College und der Emeritierung ihres Leiters, ed Herbert Lederer and Joachim Seyppel. Berlin: Die Diagonale, 1967, pp. 94-103.

H75   MENSCHING, GERHARD: *Die Kirche auf dem Theater. Shaw-Schnitzler-Brecht-Hochhuth.* In: Religion und Religionen. Festschrift für Gustav Mensching zu seinem 65. Geburtstag. Bonn: Ludwig Röhrscheid Verlag, 1967, pp. 332-345. [Discusses Schnitzler's "Professor Bernhardi"].

H76   PÜTZ, PETER: *Arthur Schnitzler und Friedrich Nietzsche.* In: P. P., Friedrich Nietzsche. Stuttgart: J. B. Metzlersche Verlagsbuchhandlung, 1967, pp. 73-74.

H77   REICHERT, HERBERT W.: *Thomas Mann on Arthur Schnitzler: Commentary on Two Eulogies.* In: JIASRA, 6, iv (1967), 13-15.

H78   REY, WILLIAM H.: *Schnitzlers Erzählung "Casanovas Heimfahrt." Eine Strukturanalyse.* In: Festschrift für Bernhard Blume, ed. Egon Schwarz, Hunter G. Hannum and Edgar Lohner. Göttingen: Vandenhoeck & Ruprecht, 1967 pp. 195-217.

H79   REIDER, HEINZ: *Die Literatur der Seele. Von Arthur Schnitzler zu George Saiko.* In: ÖGL, 11, iii (1967), 134-150.

H80 RÜHLE, GÜNTHER: *Theater für die Republik 1917-1933 im Spiegel der Kritik.* Frankfurt a.M.: S. Fischer Verlag, 1967. [Pp. 278-282: "Reigen." Brief note by G. R. and feuilletons by Alfred Kerr (first in "Berliner Tageblatt," Dec. 24, 1920), Herbert Ihering (first in "Berliner Börsen-Courier," Dec. 24, 1920), Ludwig Sternaux (first in "Berliner Lokal-Anzeiger," Dec. 24, 1920) and Paul Wiegler (first in "BZ am Mittag, Berlin," Dec. 24, 1920].

H81 SCHNETZ, DIETMUT: *Der moderne Einakter. Eine poetologische Untersuchung.* Bern: Francke Verlag, 1967, 244 p. [Pp. 35 f.: "Der grüne Kakadu." Also mentions other Schnitzler works].
Reviewed by:
H81.1 Hannum, Hunter G. In: Monatshefte, 62, i (1970), 77-79.

H82 STROKA, ANNA: *Die Gesellschaftskritik in Arthur Schnitzlers frühen Bühnenwerken.* In: GW, 11 (1967), 41-56.

H83 SWALES, M. W.: *Arthur Schnitzler as a Moralist.* In: MLR, 62, iii (1967), 462-475.

H84 VOLKE, WERNER: *Hugo von Hofmannsthal in Selbstzeugnissen und Bilddokumenten.* Reinbek bei Hamburg: Rowohlt Taschenbuch Verlag, 1967. [Numerous references to Schnitzler].

H85 WALKER, WARREN S.: *Arthur Schnitzler.* In: W. W., Twentieth Century Short Story Explication. Interpretations, 1900-1966, of Short Fiction Since 1800. 2nd Edition. Hamden: The Shoe String Press, 1967, pp. 600-601. [Bibliographical reference for selected works].

H86 ZOHN, HARRY: *Three Austrian Jews in German Literature: Schnitzler, Zweig, Herzl.* In: The Jews of Austria. Essays on their Life, History and Destruction, ed. Josef Fraenkel. London: Vallentine Mitchell, 1967, pp. 67-81.

1968

H87 Anonymous: *Surgeon of the Soul* [Arthur Schnitzler]. In: MD. Medical Newsmagazine, 12, vii (1968), 154-158. [For the non-German reader: helpful summary of the life and work of Schnitzler].

H88 BAULAND, PETER: *The Hooded Eagle. Modern German Drama on the New York Stage.* New York: Syracuse University Press, 1968. [Schnitzler: pp. 26-31, 56-57, 173-175, and passim; based on P. B.'s 1964 dissertation].

H89 BENTLEY, ERIC: *Reigen Comes Full Circle.* In: E. B., What is Theater? New York: Atheneum, 1968, pp. 152-155. [Reprinted from E. B.'s 1954 "The Dramatic Event: An American Chronicle"].

H90 BINION, RUDOLF: *Frau Lou. Nietzsche's Wayward Disciple.* Princeton: Princeton University Press, 1968, 587 p. [Pp. 190-200 and passim: Schnitzler — Frau Lou relationship (including passages from Schnitzler diaries].

H91 CHEVAL, RENÉ: *Roman Rollands Begegnungen mit Österreich.* Innsbruck: Innsbrucker Beiträge zur Kulturwissenschaft, 1968. [Pp. 12-13: Schnitzler, Rolland and Zweig].

H92 CHIAVACCI, VINZENZ K.: *Karl Schönherr und seine Zeit. Ein Lebensbild.* In: Karl Schönherr. Gesamtausgabe: Lyrik und Prosa. Ed. V. K. C. Wien: Georg Müller Verlag, 1968, pp. 7-144.

H93 CYSARZ, HERBERT: *Das Imaginäre in der Dichtung Arthur Schnitzlers.* In: MAL, 1, iii (1968), 7-17. [Also in: Wissenschaft und Weltbild, 13, ii (1960), 102-112].

H94 DIERSCH, MANFRED: *Nachwort.* In: Arthur Schnitzler, Dramen. Berlin: Aufbau Verlag, 1968.

H95 DOPPLER, ALFRED: *Dramatische Formen bei Arthur Schnitzler.* In: Beiträge zur Dramatik Österreichs im 20. Jahrhundert, ed. Institut für Österreichkunde. Wien: Verlag Ferdinand Hirt, 1968, pp. 17-30.

H96 *Hugo von Hofmannsthal – Leopold von Andrian Briefwechsel.* Ed. Walter H. Perl. Frankfurt a.M.: S. Fischer Verlag, 1968, 527 p. [Numerous references to Schnitzler].

H97 JUST, GOTTFRIED: *Ironie und Sentimentalität in den erzählenden Dichtungen Arthur Schnitzlers.* Berlin: Erich Schmidt Verlag, 1968, 149 p.
Reviewed by:
H97.1 Bauer, W.M. In: DLZ, 90 (1969), 1085-1087.
H97.2 Derré, Françoise. In: EG, 25 i (1970) 116-118.
H97.3 Kimpel, Dieter. In: Germanistik, 10, iv (1969), 917.
H97.4 LoCicero, Vincent. In: MAL, 2, iv (1969), 48-51.
H97.5 Majut, Rudolf. In: GRM, 20, i (1970), 114-115.
H97.6 Swales, Martin. In: MLR, 45, i (1970), 223-224.

H98 KINDERMANN, HEINZ: *Theatergeschichte Europas. Naturalismus und Impressionismus.* Bd. VIII (1. Teil) & Bd. IX (2. Teil). Salzburg: Otto Müller Verlag, 1968 & 1970.

H99 KLARMANN, ADOLF D.: *Arthur Schnitzler und wir.* In: MAL, 1, ii (1968), 9-27.

H100 LOTHAR, ERNST: *Rede zum Gedächtnis Arthur Schnitzlers. Gehalten im Burgtheater anläßlich des 100. Geburtstages am 15. Mai 1962.* In: E. L., Macht und Ohnmacht des Theaters. Reden, Regeln, Rechenschaft. Wien: Paul Zsolnay Verlag, 1968, pp. 27-40.

H101 ––––––: *Ein Arzt am Scheideweg. Schnitzlers "Professor Bernhardi."* In: E. L., Macht und Ohnmacht des Theaters. Reden, Regeln, Rechenschaft. Wien: Paul Zsolnay Verlag, 1968, pp. 155-158.

H102 ––––––––: *Schnitzler oder die zweifache Dämonie. Zu den Einaktern "Die Gefährtin," "Lebendige Stunden," "Komtesse Mizzi."* In: E. L., Macht und Ohnmacht des Theaters. Reden, Regeln, Rechenschaft. Wien: Paul Zsolnay Verlag, 1968, pp. 178-181.

H103   MAJUT, RUDOLF: Rev. of *Studies in Arthur Schnitzler*, ed.
       Herbert W. Reichert and Hermann Salinger. Chapel Hill: University
       of North Carolina Press, 1963, 116 p. In: GRM, 18, ii (1968),
       203-205

H104   MELCHINGER, CHRISTA: *Illusion und Wirklichkeit im
       dramatischen Werk Arthur Schnitzlers.* Heidelberg: Carl Winter
       Universitätsverlag, 1968, 138 p.
       Reviewed by:
       H104.1 Bauer, Wolfgang M. In: DLZ, 92, (1971), 885-888.
       H104.2 LoCicero, Vincent. In: MAL, 2, iv (1969), 51-54.
       H104.3 Swales, Martin. In: MLR, 45, iii (1970), 706-707.
       H104.4 Williams, Cedric E. In: GL&L, 25, ii (1972), 171-172.
       H104.5 Žmegač, Viktor. In: Germanistik, 11, ii (1970), 401.

H105   NARDROFF, ERNEST HENRY VON: *Doktor Gräsler, Badearzt:
       Weather as an aspect of Schnitzler's symbolism.* In: GR, 43, ii
       (1968), 109-120.

H106   PALMER, HELEN H. and ANNE J. DYSON: *Arthur Schnitzler.* In:
       H. P. & A. D., European Drama Criticism. Hamden: The Shoe String
       Press, 1968, pp. 362-366. [Bibliographical reference for selected
       works].

H107   POLITZER, HEINZ: *Diagnose und Dichtung. Zum Werk Arthur
       Schnitzlers.* In: H. P., Das Schweigen der Sirenen: Studien zur
       deutschen und österreichischen Literatur. Stuttgart: J. B.
       Metzlersche Verlagsbuchhandlung, 1968, pp. 110-141. [First in:
       Forum (Wien), 9, ci (1962), 217-219; 9, cii (1962), 266-270].

H108   PRANG, HELMUT: *Arthur Schnitzler.* In: H. P., Geschichte des
       Lustspiels. Stuttgart: Alfred Kröner Verlag, 1968, pp. 276-281.
       [Discusses Schnitzler's "Anatol", "Der grüne Kakadu", "Literatur",
       "Zwischenspiel", "Zum großen Wurstel", "Professor Bernhardi"].

H109   REICH-RANICKI, MARCEL: *Schnitzler über Schnitzler. Die
       fragwürdige Selbstdarstellung eines Meisters unserer Literatur.* In:
       Die Zeit, 23, 47 (1968).

H110   REY, WILLIAM H.: *Arthur Schnitzler: Die späte Prosa als Gipfel
       seines Schaffens.* Berlin: Erich Schmidt Verlag, 1968, 198 p.
       Reviewed by:
       H110.1 Angress, Ruth K. In: Monatshefte, 62, iv (1970), 412-413.
       H110.2 Bauer, W.M. In: DLZ, 90 (1969), 998-1000.
       H110.3 Coghlan, Brian. In: Journal of the Australasian Universities
       Language and Literature Association, 34 (1970), 354-355.
       H110.4 Cohn, Hilde D. In: GQ, 43, ii (1970), 289-290.
       H110.5 Derré, Françoise. In: EG, 25, i (1970), 116-118.
       H110.6 Klarmann, Adolf D. In: Modern Language Quarterly, 33, iii
       (1972), 343-346.
       H110.7 Konrad, G. In: Wort und Wahrheit, 24 (1969), 224.

H110.8 LoCicero, Vincent. In: MAL, 2, iv (1969), 46-48.

H110.9 Plant, Richard. In: GR, 46, i (1971), 81-83.

H110.10 Surowska, B. In: Weimarer Beiträge, 17, ii (1971), 220-221.

H110.11 Swales, Martin. In: MLR, 45, i (1970), 224-225.

H111   RIEDER, HEINZ: *Österreichische Moderne: Studien zum Weltbild und Menschenbild in ihrer Epik und Lyrik.* Bonn: H. Bouvier u. Co. Verlag, 1968, pp. 40-44. [Schnitzler influenced by Freud; "Leutnant Gustl"].

H112   SANDERS, JON BARRY: *Arthur Schnitzler's "Reigen": Lost Romanticism.* In: MAL, 1, iv (1968), 56-66.

H113   SCHICK, ALFRED: *The Vienna of Sigmund Freud.* In: The Psychoanalytic Review, 55, iv (1968-1969), 529-551.

H114   SCHLEIN, RENA R.: *Arthur Schnitzler: Author-Scientist.* In: MAL, 1, ii (1968), 28-38.

H115   STROKA, ANNA: *Der Impressionismus in Arthur Schnitzlers "Anatol" und seine gesellschaftlichen und ideologischen Voraussetzungen.* In: GW, 12, lxxvi (1968), 97-111.

H116   THIEBERGER, RICHARD: *Introduction.* In: Arthur Schnitzler, Die Toten schweigen und andere Erzählungen, ed. Robin Sawers. London: George G. Harrap & Co., 1968, pp. 7-16. [Historical/sociological discussion of selected works].

H117   TORBERG, FRIEDRICH: *Nachwort.* In: Arthur Schnitzler, "Jugend in Wien. Eine Autobiographie", ed. Therese Nickl and Heinrich Schnitzler. Wien: Verlag Fritz Molden, 1968, pp. 330-338. (Evaluation of Schnitzler as man and author.)

H118   TRAMER, HANS: *Arthur Schnitzlers Altenberg-Stück.* In: Bulletin des Leo Baeck Instituts, 11, xlii (1968), 125-152.

H119   URBACH, REINHARD: *Arthur Schnitzler.* (First Edition.) Velber bei Hannover: Friedrich Verlag, 1968, 134 p.
        Reviewed by:
        H119.1 Derré, Françoise. In: Germanistik, 10, i (1969), 206.
        H119.2 Weiss, Robert O. In: BA, 43, ii (1969), 262.

H120   ——————: "Schwätzer sind Verbrecher": Bemerkungen zu Schnitzlers Dramenfragment "Das Wort". In: LuK, 25 (1968), 292-304.

H121   ——————: *Teil und Gegenteil.* In: Neues Forum, 15 (1968), 791.

H122   ——————: *Gedanken und Bedenken. Arthur Schnitzlers Aphorismen und Betrachtungen.* In: Neue Wege. Kulturschrift junger Menschen. Nr. 232, Jg. 24 (Dezember, 1968), 9-11.

H123   WEISS, ROBERT O.: *The Psychoses in the Works of Arthur Schnitzler:* In: GQ, 41, iii (1968), 377-400.

H124   WILPERT, GERO VON and ADOLF GÜHRING: *Schnitzler.* In: G. v. W. and A. G., Erstausgaben Deutscher Dichtung: Eine Bibliographie zur deutschen Literatur, 1600-1960. Stuttgart: Alfred Kröner Verlag, 1968, pp. 1148-1149.

H125 ALEXANDER, THEODOR W. and BEATRICE W.: *Schnitzler's "Leutnant Gustl" and Dujardin's "Les Lauriers sont coupés"*. In: MAL, 2, ii (1969), 7-15.

H126 BAREIKIS, ROBERT: *Arthur Schnitzler's "Fräulein Else": A Freudian Novelle?* In: L&P, 19, i (1969), 19-32

H127 BOECK, JOH. A.: *Vorwort*. In: Arthur Schnitzler, Ausgew. Werke: Liebelei und andere Bühnenwerke. Wien: Buchgem. Donauland, 1969.

H128 COHN, DORRITT: *Erlebte Rede im Ich-Roman*. In: GRM, 19, iii (1969), 304-313. [Pp. 310-311 discuss Schnitzler].

H129 *Das Erscheinungsbild der österreichischen Gegenwartsdichtung*, ed. Leo Kober. Wien: Wilhelm Braumüller, 1969, 158 p.

H130 FARESE, GIUSEPPE: *Individuo e società nel romanzo "Der Weg ins Freie" di Arthur Schnitzler*. Rome: Bulzoni, 1969, 241 p.
Reviewed by:
H130.1 Aspetsberger, Friedbert. In: Germanistik, 12, i (1971), 180.
H130.2 Ricci, J. F. A. In: EG, 29, ii (1974), 260-261.

H131 FRIEDRICHSMEYER, ERHARD: *Schnitzlers "Der grüne Kakadu"*. In: ZDP, 88, ii (1969), 209-228.

H132 ──────: *Bemerkungen zum Heldischen bei Schnitzler*. In: MAL, 2, iv (1969), 38-41.

H133 HEINDL, GOTTFRIED: *Und die Größe ist gefährlich. Oder wahrhaftige Geschichten zur Geschichte eines schwierigen Volks*. Wien: Paul Neff Verlag, 1969, p. 170. [Anecdote about Schnitzler].

H134 KATAN, M.: *Schnitzler's "Das Schicksal des Freiherrn von Leisenbohg."* In: Journal of the American Psychoanalytic Association, 17, iii (1969), 904-926.

H135 KERNER, W.: *Der Arzt im Werk Arthur Schnitzler*. In: Hippokrates. Zeitschrift für praktische Heilkunde, 40, xx (1969), 803-807.

H136 KONRAD, GUSTAV: *Arthur Schnitzler als Erzähler*. In: Welt und Wort, 24, iv (1969), 112.

H137 KRUNTORAD, PAUL: *Literatur und Liebelei*. In: Forum (Wien), 16 (1969), 743-744.

H138 LEDERER, HERBERT: *Vorwort*. In: Arthur Schnitzler. Frühe Gedichte, ed. Herbert Lederer. Berlin: Propyläen Verlag, 1969, pp. 7-12. [Introduction to the poems].

H139 LINDKEN, HANS-ULRICH: *Arthur Schnitzler: Spiel im Morgengrauen*. In: ÖGL, 13, viii (1969), 407-426.

H140 LoCICERO, VINCENT: *A Study of Persona in Selected Works of Arthur Schnitzler*. In: MAL, 2, iv (1969), 7-29.

H141 NEHRING, WOLFGANG: *"Schluck und Jau." Impressionismus bei Gerhart Hauptmann*. In: ZDP, 88, ii (1969), 189-209. [Suggests possible influence of Schnitzler on Hauptmann].

H142 NEUMANN, GERHARD and JUTTA MÜLLER: *Der Nachlass Arthur Schnitzlers.* Munich: Wilhelm Fink Verlag, 1969, 200 p. Reviewed by:
H142.1 Kluge, Gerhard. In: Germanistik, 11, iv (1970), 829-830.

H143 NOLTENIUS, RAINER: *Hofmannsthal-Schröder-Schnitzler: Möglichkeiten und Grenzen des modernen Aphorismus.* Stuttgart: J. B. Metzlersche Verlagsbuchhandlung, 1969, 256 p. Reviewed by:
H143.1 Neumann, Gerhard. In: Germanistik, 11, ii (1970), 371-372.

H143.2 Swales, Martin. In: BA, 45, i (1971), 122.

H144 REICHERT, HERBERT: *The Hero in Schnitzler's Dramas.* In: MAL, 2, iv (1969), 42-45.

H145 REY, WILLIAM H.: *Arthur Schnitzler.* In: Deutsche Dichter der Moderne: Ihr Leben und Werk, ed. Benno von Wiese. 2nd Edition. Berlin: Erich Schmidt Verlag, 1969, pp. 241-261.

H146 SCHLEIN, RENA R.: *The Motif of Hypocrisy in the Works of Arthur Schnitzler.* In: MAL, 2, i (1969), 28-38.

H147 SCHNEIDER, GERD K.: *Ton- und Schriftsprache in Schnitzler's "Fräulein Else" and Schumanns "Carnival".* In: MAL, 2, iii (1969), 17-20.

H148 SEITA, FUMITAKE: *Mori Ōgai and Arthur Schnitzler.* In: Hikaku Bungaku. Journal of Comparative Literature, 12 (1969), 48-56. [In Japanese. English summary, p. xv: "interpretation of Schnitzler from viewpoint of 'Entsagung';" cf. 1973 study by R. J. Bowring].

H149 SINGER, HERBERT: *Arthur Schnitzler: "Der grüne Kakadu".* In: Das deutsche Lustspiel II, ed. Hans Steffen. Göttingen: Vandenhoeck & Ruprecht, 1969, pp. 61-78.

H150 STERN, GUY: *Brechts "Trommeln in der Nacht" als literarische Satire.* In: Monatshefte, 61, iii (1969), 241-259. [P. 254: suggestion that Brecht may have been influenced by Schnitzler].

H151 STROKA, ANNA: *Arthur Schnitzlers Einakter "Paracelsus", "Die Gefährtin", und "Der grüne Kakadu".* In: GW, 13, cx (1969), 57-66.

H152 URBACH, REINHARD: *Sterbensworte und Lebenslügen.* In: Neue Blätter des Theaters in der Josefstadt, 4 (1969).

H153 WEISS, ROBERT O.: *The "Hero" in Schnitzler's Comedy "Professor Bernhardi".* In: MAL, 2, iv (1969), 30-33.

1970

H154 ALLEN, RICHARD H.: *"79 Personen": Character Relationships in Schnitzler's "Der junge Medardus".* In: Studies in German Literature of the Nineteenth and Twentieth Centuries: Festschrift for Frederic E. Coenen. Chapel Hill: University of North Carolina Press, 1970, pp. 149-156.

H155 ASPETSBERGER, FRIEDBERT: *Wiener Dichtung der Jahrhundertwende. Beobachtungen zu Schnitzlers und Hofmannsthals Kunstformen.* In: Studi Germanici, 8, iii (1970), 410-451.

H156 BAUMANN, GERHART: *Nachwort.* In: Arthur Schnitzler, "Anatol", "Anatols Größenwahn", "Der grüne Kakadu", ed. Gerhart Baumann. Stuttgart: Philipp Reclam, 1970, pp. 157-173. [Discussion of "Anatol" and "Der grüne Kakadu].

H157 ——————: *Arthur Schnitzler.* In: Handbuch der deutschen Gegenwartsliteratur, ed. Hermann Kunisch. München: Nymphenburger Verlagshandlung, 1970, pp. 187-190. [Also translated into English. See 1973 listing].

H158 BERLIN, JEFFREY B.: *"Forgotten" Schnitzler Dissertations.* In: MAL, 3, iv (1970), 68. [Mentions five dissertations not included in Allen's bibliography].

H159 CAZDEN, ROBERT E.: *German Exile Literature in America: 1933-1950.* Chicago: American Library Association, 1970. [P. 88, n. 52: Schnitzler listed twelfth in popularity of German authors read in America before 1941].

H160 DERRÉ, FRANÇOISE: *Einleitung.* In: Arthur Schnitzler, "Zug der Schatten", ed. Françoise Derré. Frankfurt a.M.: S. Fischer Verlag, 1970, pp. 5-16.

H161 DICKERSON, HAROLD D. Jr.: *Arthur Schnitzler's "Die Frau des Richters": A Statement of Futility* In: GQ, 43, ii (1970), 223-236.

H162 ELLENBERGER, HENRI F.: *The Discovery of the Unconscious: The History and Evolution of Dynamic Psychiatry.* New York: Basic Books. 1970. [Pp. 471-474: differences between Freud and Schnitzler].

H163 FONTANA, OSKAR MAURUS: *Es war wie bei Schnitzler.* In: Wiener Unsterblichkeiten, ed. O. M. F. Ergänzt und neu herausgegeben von Erik G. Wickenburg. München: Lagen – Müller Verlag, 1970, pp. 132-135. [Recollection of Schnitzler's burial; contains significant biographical information. First appeared in Das Tagebuch, 12-2, xliv, Oct. 31, 1931, 1707-1709; republished in 1958 edition of Wiener Unsterblichkeiten].

H164 GRAF, HANSJÖRG: *Nachwort.* In: Der kleine Salon. Szenen und Prosa des Wiener Fin de Siècle. Mit Illustrationen von Gustav Klimt. Ed. H. G. Stuttgart: Goverts Krüger Stahlberg Verlag, 1970, pp. 286-300. [General introduction to Schnitzler's time period. Also contains (pp. 7-47) Schnitzler's "Die kleine Komödie."].

H165 GRÖGL, GERTRAUD: *Arthur Schnitzlers Entwicklung zum doctor poeta.* In: Jahresbericht 1969/70: Bundesgymnasium Wien 8 (Piaristen-Gymnasium). Wien: Gustaf Adolf Neumann Ges., pp. 9-18. [Contains biographical material from the *Nachlaß*].

H166   GROTE, MARIE: *Themes and Variations in the Early Prose Fiction of Arthur Schnitzler.* In: MAL, 3, iv (1970), 22-47.

H167   *Handbuch zur modernen Literatur im Deutschunterricht,* ed. Paul Dormagen, Fritz Gieselmann et. al. Frankfurt a.M.: Hirschgraben-Verlag, 1970, pp. 17-19. [Plot summaries of "Der blinde Geronimo und sein Bruder", "Die Hirtenflöte", "Leutnant Gustl", and "Der grüne Kakadu"].

H168   HAUSNER, HARRY H.: *Die Beziehungen zwischen Arthur Schnitzler und Sigmund Freud.* In: MAL, 3, ii (1970), 48-61.

H169   KESTING, MARIANNE: *Arthur Schnitzler.* In: M. K., Entdeckung und Destruktion: Zur Strukturwandlung der Künste. Munich: Wilhelm Fink Verlag, 1970, pp. 123-141.
Reviewed by:
H169.1 Lockemann, Wolfgang. In: GQ, 46, iii (1973), 474-478.

H170   LEA, HENRY A.: *Werfel's Unfinished Novel: Saga of the Marginal Jew.* In: Germanic Review, 45, ii (1970). [P. 107, n. 4: Werfel's "Cella oder die Überwinder: Versuch eines Romans" and Schnitzler's "Der Weg ins Freie"].

H171   LINDKEN, HANS ULRICH: *Interpretationen zu Arthur Schnitzler.* Munich: R. Oldenbourg Verlag, 1970, 112 p. [Examination of "Spiel im Morgengrauen", "Der blinde Geronimo und sein Bruder" and "Leutnant Gustl"].
Reviewed by:
H171.1 Bauer, Werner M. In: Sprachkunst, 2, iv (1971), 403-405.
H171.2 Doppler, Alfred. In: ÖGL, 17, ii (1973), 134.
H171.3 Morewedge, Rosmarie T. In: MAL, 6, iii/iv (1973), 259-262.

H172   MENDELSSOHN, PETER DE: *S. Fischer und sein Verlag.* Frankfurt a.M.: S. Fischer Verlag, 1970, 1487 p. [Highly valuable reference work that includes much new information].

H173   MORTON, FREDERIC: *Forward.* In: Arthur Schnitzler, "My Youth in Vienna", tr. Catherine Hutter. New York: Holt, Rinehart and Winston, Inc., 1970, pp. ix-xiv. [Historical/sociological discussion].

H174   MÜHLHER, ROBERT: *Das "Historische" als Baustein der österreichischen Moderne.* In: Geschichte in der österreichischen Literatur des 19. und 20. Jahrhunderts. Ed. Institut für Österreichkunde. Wien: Verlag Ferdinand Hirt, 1970, pp. 93-109. [See esp. pp. 100-104: Hofmannsthal's prologue to "Anatol"].
Reviewed by:
H174.1 Frank, Peter R. In: Germanistik, 14, ii (1973), 348-349.

H175   OFFERMANNS, ERNST L.: *Arthur Schnitzlers Komödie "Fink und Fliederbusch".* In: MAL, 3, ii (1970), 7-24.

H176 PERL, WALTER H.: *Der Dichter Leopold Andrian: Frühvollendung und Verstummen.* In: Philobiblon, 14, i (1970), 49-56. [Shortened version in: MAL, 2, ii (1969), 23-29].

H177 SCHEIBLE, HARTMUT: *Diskretion und Verdrängung zu Schnitzlers Autobiographie.* In: FH, 25, (1970), 129-134.

H178 SEIDLIN, OSKAR: *Arthur Schnitzler – in Retrospect.* In: Festschrift für Detlev W. Schumann zum 70. Geburtstag, ed. Albert R. Schmitt. Munich: Delp'sche Verlagsbuchhandlung, 1970, pp. 319-324. [Brief revision of an earlier study: "In Memoriam Arthur Schnitzler," AGR, 28, iv (1962), 4-6].

H179 WAGNER, RENATE: *Arthur Schnitzlers Beziehung zu Otto Brahm und zu Max Reinhardt: Zu zwei Briefwechseln des Dichters.* In: Neue Zürcher Zeitung, Nr. 425, Sept. 13, 1970.

H180 WALTON, LUVERNE: *"Anatol" on the New York Stage.* In: MAL, 2, ii (1969), 30-44.

H181 WEIGEL, HANS: *Der Offizielle Teil der Novelle. Ein Vorwort.* In: Liebe, die starb vor der Zeit. Arthur Schnitzler und Olga Waissnix. Ein Briefwechsel, ed. Therese Nickl and Heinrich Schnitzler. Wien: Verlag Fritz Molden, 1970, pp. 9-20. [Discussion of relationship between Schnitzler and Waissnix].

H182 ––––––: *Karl Kraus oder die Macht der Ohnmacht.* Wien: Verlag Fritz Molden, 1970, pp. 266-268. [Discusses Schnitzler and Kraus].

H183 ZUCKERKANDL, BERTHA: *Mein Telefon-Tagebuch* and *Arthur Schnitzlers Anfänge und ein Abschied.* In: B. Z., Österreich intim. Erinnerungen 1892-1942. Ed. Reinhard Federmann. Berlin: Propyläen Verlag, 1970, pp. 9-10 and 24-30. [Contains some biographical information and critical comments by a contemporary of Schnitzler].
Reviewed by:
H183.1 Johns, Jorun B. In: MAL, 8, iii/iv (1975), 396-398.
H183.2 Volke, Werner. In: Germanistik, 14, i (1973), 200-201.

1971

H184 ALEXANDER, THEODOR W.: *From the Scientific to the Supernatural in Schnitzler.* In: Studies by Members of SCMLA, 31, iv (1971), 164-167

H185 –––––– and BEATRICE W.: *Maupassant's "Yvette" and Schnitzler's "Fräulein Else".* In: MAL, 4, iii (1971), 44-55.

H186 ALTER, MARIA P.: *Schnitzler's Physician: An Existential Character.* In: MAL, 4, iii (1971), 7-23.

45

H187   ------: *The Concept of Physician in the Writings of Hans Carossa and Arthur Schnitzler.* Bern: Verlag Herbert Lang, 1971, 102 p.
Reviewed by:
H187.1 Dickerson, Harold D. Jr. in: MAL, 6, i/ii (1973), 199-201.
H187.2 Hinze, Klaus-Peter. In: GQ, 45, iv (1972), 732.
H187.3 Paoli, Rodolfo. In: Germanistik, 14, i (1973), 210-211.

H188   *The Arthur Schnitzler Archive.* In: MAL, 4, i (1971), 63-76.

H189   BERLIN, JEFFREY B.: *Arthur Schnitzler: A Bibliography of Criticism, 1965-1971* In: MAL, 4, iv (1971), 7-20.

H190   DICKERSON, HAROLD D. Jr.: *Water and Vision as Mystical Elements in Schnitzler's "Der Gang zum Weiher".* In: MAL, 4, iii (1971), 24-36.

H191   DOPPLER, ALFRED: *Die Problematik der Sprache und des Sprechens in den Bühnenstücken Arthur Schnitzlers.* In: Marginalien zur poetischen Welt. Festschrift für Robert Mühlher zum 60. Geburtstag, ed. Alois Eder. Berlin: Duncker und Humbolt, 1971, pp. 283-297.

H192   ------: *Arthur Schnitzler. "Leutnant Gustl."* Interpretationen zur österreichischen Literatur, ed. Institut für Österreichkunde. Wien: Verlag Ferdinand Hirt, 1971, pp. 53-61.

H193   DRIVER, BEVERLEY R.: *Arthur Schnitzler's "Frau Berta Garlan": A Study in Form.* In: GR, 46, iv (1971), 285-298.

H194   FARESE, GIUSEPPE: *Arthur Schnitzler alla luce della critica recente (1966-1970).* In: Studi Germanici, 9, i-ii (1971), 234-268.

H195   ------: *Introduction.* In: Arthur Schnitzler. Novelle. Tr. G. F. Rome: Edizioni dell'Ateneo, 1971, pp. vii-cxv.

H196   FREEMAN, ERIKA: *Insights. Conversations with Theodor Reik.* Englewood Cliffs: Prentice-Hall, Inc., 1971, 244 p. [P. 90: Reik verifies that Freud considered Schnitzler his "Doppelgänger."].

H197   GEISSLER, KLAUS: *Arthur Schnitzler und seine Darstellung des Judentums.* In: Tribüne. Zeitschrift zum Verständnis des Judentums, 10, H. 40 (1971), 4407-4415.

H198   HAJEK, EDELGARD: *Literarischer Jugendstil. Vergleichende Studien zur Dichtung und Malerei um 1900.* Düsseldorf: Bertelsmann Universitätsverlag, 1971, 117 p. [Pp. 70-72 & 77-79: "Anatol," "Die Frau mit dem Dolche," "Leutnant Gustl" and "Reigen"].
Reviewed by:
H198.1 Hermand, Jost. In: Germanistik, 14, ii (1973), 447.

H199   HENDERSON, ARCHIBALD: *Arthur Schnitzler.* In: A. H., European Dramatists. New York: Books for Libraries Press, 1971, pp. 409-465. [Reprint of 1926 edition].

H200   HOFMANNSTHAL, HUGO VON: *Über Schnitzlers "Anatol."* Ed.

Rudolf Hirsch. In: Neue Rundschau, 82, iv (1971), 795-797.

H201 IMBODEN, MICHAEL: *Die surreale Komponente im erzählenden Werk Arthur Schnitzlers.* Bern: Verlag Herbert Lang, 1971, 131 p.
Reviewed by:
H201.1 Derré, Françoise. In: Germanistik, 15, iii (1974), 729-730.
H201.2 Falk, Thomas H. In: BA, 47, i (1973), 138-139.
H201.3 Foltin, Lore B. In: GQ, 47, (1974), 108-109.
H201.4 Frye, Wendell. In: Germanic Notes, 3, iii (1972), 23.
H201.5 Kuxdorf, Manfred. In: MAL, 6, iii/iv (1973), 231-233.
H201.6 Workman, J.D. In: Monatshefte, 64, ii (1972), 165.

H202 KAUFMANN, HANS: *Fortsetzung realistischer Erzähltraditionen des 19. Jahrhunderts bei L. Thoma, A. Schnitzler, E. v. Keyserling, G. Hermann und dem frühen H. Hesse.* In: Wissenschaftliche Zeitschrift der Friedrich-Schiller-Universität Jena. Gesellschafts u. Sprachwissenschaftliche Reihe, 20 (1971), 499-512.

H203 KROTKOFF, HERTHA: *Auf den Spuren von Arthur Schnitzlers Traumnovelle.* In: MAL, 4, iv (1971), 37-41.

H204 MÜLLER-SEIDEL, WALTER: *Literatur und Ideologie. Zur Situation des deutschen Romans um 1900.* In: Dichtung — Sprache — Gesellschaft (Akten des IV. Internationalen Germanisten-Kongress 1970 in Princeton). Ed. Victor Lange and Hans-Gert Roloff. Frankfurt am Main: Athenäum Verlag, 1971. [See esp. p. 596: skepticism of language in work of Schnitzler; and pp. 598-599: Schnitzler's "Sterben"].

H205 NARDROFF, ERNEST H. VON: *Ferdinand von Saar's "Schloß Kostenitz": A Prelude to Schnitzler?* In: MAL, 4 iv (1971), 21-36.

H206 REICH-RANICKI, MARCEL: *Liebe per Sie: Arthur Schnitzlers Briefwechsel mit Olga Waissnix.* In: Allgemeine, Nr. XXVI/3, Jan. 15, 1971, 7.

H207 REID, MAJA D.: *"Die Hirtenflöte".* In: MAL, 4, ii (1971), 18-27.

H208 REY, WILLIAM H.: *Arthur Schnitzler: Professor Bernhardi.* Munich: Wilhelm Fink Verlag, 1971, 102 p.
Reviewed by:
H208.1 Derré, Françoise. In: EG, 27, iv (1972), 642-645.
H208.2 ————: In: Germanistik, 13, i (1972), 196.
H208.3 Howarth, Peter. In: MAL, 6, i/ii (1973), 188-192.
H208.4 Klarmann, Adolf D. In: MLQ, 33, iii (1972), 343-346.
H208.5 Schlein, Rena R. In: Monatshefte, 65, ii (1973), 194-196.
H208.6 Swales, Martin. In: GL&L, 27, ii (1974), 163-164.

H209 STROKA, ANNA: *Arthur Schnitzlers Tragikomödien.* In: GW, 14, (1971), 55-73.

H210 SWALES, MARTIN: *Arthur Schnitzler: A Critical Study.* London: Oxford University Press, 1971, 289 p.
Reviewed by:
H210.1 Beharriell, Frederick J. In: JEGP, 72, iii (1973), 424-428.
H210.2 Burkhard, Arthur. In: MLN, 87, v (1972), 799-800.
H210.3 Derré, Françoise. In: EG, 27, iv (1972), 642-645.
H210.4 Fischer, Jens M. In: Germanistik, 13, ii (1972), 404.
H210.5 Jacobs, Margaret. In: GL&L, 28, ii (1975), 178.
H210.6 Schmidt, Willa. In: Monatshefte, 64, iii (1972), 317-318.
H210.7 Schneider, Gerd. In: MAL, 5, iii/iv (1972), 142-146.
H211 TÖRÖK, ANDREAS: *Der Liebestod bei Arthur Schnitzler: Eine Entlehnung von Richard Wagner.* In: MAL, 4, i (1971), 57-59.
H212 WAGNER, RENATE and BRIGITTE VACHA: *Wiener Schnitzler-Aufführungen 1891-1970.* München: Prestel-Verlag, 1971, · 183 p.
Reviewed by:
H212.1 haj [Hansres Jacobi]. In: NZZ, Nr. 412 (Sept. 5, 1971).
H213 ───────: *Einleitung.* In: Der Briefwechsel Arthur Schnitzlers mit Max Reinhardt und dessen Mitarbeiten, ed. Renate Wagner. Salzburg: Otto Müller Verlag, 1971, pp. 5-39.

1972

H214 ALBRECHT, GÜNTER and GÜNTHER DAHLKE, eds.: *Arthur Schnitzler.* In: Internationale Bibliographie zur Geschichte der deutschen Literatur von den Anfängen bis zur Gegenwart, Teil 2, 2, ed. G. A. and G. D. Berlin and München-Pullach: Verlag Dokumentation, 1972, pp. 787-793. [Lists many titles already in Allen or Berlin bibliography; significant for numerous references to Russian, Rumanian, Polish, etc. studies on Schnitzler].
H215 BAUMANN, GERHART: *Arthur Schnitzler: Spiel-Figur und Gesellschafts-Spiel.* In: G.B., Vereinigungen. Versuche zu neuerer Dichtung. Munich: Wilhelm Fink Verlag, 1972, pp. 145-172.
H216 BAYERDÖRFER, HANS-PETER: *Vom Konversationsstück zur Wurstelkomödie. Zu Arthur Schnitzlers Einaktern.* In: Jahrbuch der Deutschen Schillergesellschaft, 16 (1972), 516-575.
H217 BERLIN, JEFFREY B.: *Some Images of the Betrayer in Arthur Schnitzler's Work.* In: GL&L, 26, i (1972), 20-24.
H218 BOA, ELIZABETH and J.H. REID: *Critical Strategies: German Fiction in the Twentieth Century.* Montreal: McQuill-Queen's Press, 1972, 206 p. [Comments on "Leutnant Gustl"].
H219 COOK, WILLIAM K.: *Arthur Schnitzler's "Der blinde Geronimo und sein Bruder."* In: MAL, 5, iii/iv (1972), 120-137.

H220   COUCH, LOTTE S.: *Der Reigen: Schnitzler und Sigmund Freud.* In: ÖGL, 16, vi (1972), 217-227.

H221   DAVIAU, DONALD G. and JORUN B. JOHNS: *Introduction.* In: The Correspondence of Arthur Schnitzler and Raoul Auernheimer with Raoul Auernheimer's Aphorisms, ed. D. G. D. and J. B. J. Chapel Hill: University of North Carolina Press, 1972, pp. 3-21.

H222   DOMANDI, AGNES K., ed.: *Arthur Schnitzler.* In: Modern German Litearture. A Library of Literary Criticism. New York: Ungar Publishing Co., 1972, pp. 242-252. [Contains selections from appraisals of Schnitzler's work by various critics; presented in English translation].

H223   HEGER, ROLAND: *Der österreichische Roman des 20. Jahrhunderts.* 1. Teil. Wien: Wilhelm Braumüller, 1972, esp. pp. 138-140.

H224   HERMAND, JOST and RICHARD HAMANN: *Impressionismus.* München: Nymphenburger Verlagshandlung, 1972, 376 p. [Contains several references to Schnitzler].

H225   *Hugo von Hofmannsthal – Richard Beer-Hofmann Briefwechsel.* Ed. Eugene Weber. Frankfurt a.M.: S. Fischer Verlag, 1972, 264 p. [Numerous references to Schnitzler].

H226   JOHNSTON, WILLIAM M.: *The Austrian Mind. An Intellectual and Social History, 1848-1938* Berkeley: University of California Press, 1972, pp. 171-173 and passim.
Reviewed by:
H226.1 Klarmann, Adolf. In: Monatshefte, 66, iii (1974), 328-330.
H226.2 Zohn, Harry. In: MAL, 5, iii/iv (1972), 138-141.

H227   KILIAN, KLAUS: *Die Komödien Arthur Schnitzlers. Sozialer Rollenzwang und kritische Ethik.* Düsseldorf: Bertelsmann . Universitätsverlag, 1972, 180 p.
Reviewed by:
H227.1 Doswald, Herman K. In: MAL, 6, i/ii (1973), 193-194.
H227.2 Kuttenkeuler, Wolfgang. In: Germanistik, 13, iii (1972), 558.
H227.3 Schrimpf, Hans Joachim. In: MAL, 3, iv (1970), 61-63.

H228   KOCH, HANS-ALBRECHT: *Ein Matthias-Claudius-Zitat bei Arthur Schnitzler.* In: GRM, 22, iv (1972), 435-436.

H229   KROTKOFF, HERTHA: *Themen, Motive und Symbole in Arthur Schnitzlers "Traumnovelle."* In: MAL, 5, i/ii (1972), 70-95.

H230   LEBENSAFT, ELISABETH: *Anordnung und Funktion zentraler Aufbauelemente in den Erzahlungen Arthur Schnitzlers.* Wien: Verlag Notring, 1972, 184 p. [1970 dissertation, Universität Wien].
Reviewed by:
230.1 Goltschnigg, Dietmar. In: ÖGL, 18, iv (1974), 255-256.

H231   LIPTZIN, SOL: *A History of Yiddish Literature*. New York: Jonathan David Publishers, 1972. [P. 87: Schnitzler – David Pinski relationship; pp. 165-167: Schnitzler – H.J. Haimowitz relationship].

H232   LOTHAR, ERNST: *Schnitzler und Kanzler Seipel.* In: Aufbau. Reconstruction Dokumente einer Kultur im Exil, ed. Will Schaber. New York: Overbrook Press, 1972, pp. 340-341. [Reprinted from "Aufbau" June 6, 1941].

H233   NEUSE, ERNA: *Die Funktion von Motiven und Stereotypen Wendungen in Schnitzlers 'Reigen.'* In: Monatshefte, 64, iv (1972), 356-370.

H234   PLAUT, RICHARD: *Die Welt "entdeckt" Arthur Schnitzler.* In: Aufbau. Reconstruction Dokumente einer Kultur im Exil, ed. Will Schaber. New York: Overbrook Press, 1972, pp. 310-312. [Reprinted from "Aufbau" Nov. 29, 1968].

H235   REID, MAJA D.: *"Andreas Thameyers letzter Brief" and "Der letzte Brief eines Literaten": Two Neglected Schnitzler Stories.* In: GQ, 42, iii (1972), 443-460.

H236   SCHEIBLE, HARTMUT: *"Professor Bernhardi": Tragödie des Individuums.* In: Programmheft der Aufführung des Bayrischen Staatsschauspiels im Residenztheater. München, 1972.

H237   SCHNITZLER, HEINRICH: *Letter to Jon D. Green.* In: Jon D. Green, "The Impact of Musical Theme and Structure on the Meaning and Dramatic Unity of Selected Works by Arthur Schnitzler," Ph.D. Diss. Syracuse University, 1972. Summary in: DA, xxxiii, i (1972), 312 A. [P. 178. Letter dated March 7, 1971: briefly discusses some aspects of his father's position toward music].

H238   *Heinrich Schnitzler – Biographische Daten.* Ed. Reinhard Urbach. In: Neue Blätter des Theaters in der Josefstadt. 1972. [Contains brief discussion of the major events in the life of Arthur Schnitzler's son and biographical notations].

H239   SPIEL, HILDE: *Fragmente. Schnitzlers "Zug der Schatten" im Wiener Volkstheater.* In: Theater heute, 13, ii (1972), 20.

H240   SWALES, MARTIN: *Introduction: I. Arthur Schnitzler's Vienna. II. "Professor Bernhardi" As A Comedy.* In: Arthur Schnitzler, "Professor Bernhardi," ed. M. S. New York: Pergamon Press, 1972, pp. 1-20.
Reviewed by:
H240.1 Schlein, Rena R. In: MAL, 6, iii/iv (1973), 255-256.

H241   TÖRÖK, ANDREW: *"Der Weg ins Freie": Versuch einer Neuinterpretation.* In: Monatshefte, 64, iv (1972), 371-377.

H242   URBACH, REINHARD: *Arthur Schnitzler.* 2nd Edition. Velber bei Hannover: Friedrich Verlag, 1972, 143 p.

H243   VIERECK, GEORGE S.: *The World of Arthur Schnitzler.* In: MAL, 5, iii/iv (1972), 7-17. [Reprint of 1930 interview with Schnitzler].

H244   WEIGEL, HANS: *Ein treuer Diener des Theaters. Vorweggenommener Geburtstagsgruß für Heinrich Schnitzler.* (On the occasion of Heinrich Schnitzler's seventieth birthday). In: Neue Blätter des Theaters in der Josefstadt. 1972.

H245   WEISS, ROBERT O.: *The Human Element in Arthur Schnitzler's Social Criticism.* In: MAL, 5, i/ii (1972), 30-44.

H245a   ——————: *Introduction. I. Arthur Schnitzler: A Profile. II. Some of Schnitzler's Work and Thought as Indices of His Development. III. Some Day Peace Will Return: Notes on War and Peace.* In: Arthur Schnitzler, Some Day Peace Will Return. Notes on War and Peace, ed. and tr. by Robert O. Weiss. New York: Frederick Ungar, 1972, pp. 3-31.

H246   ——————: *Introduction.* In: Arthur Schnitzler, The Mind in Words and Actions. Preliminary Remarks Concerning Two Diagrams, tr. by Robert O. Weiss. New York: Frederick Ungar, 1972, pp. vii-xv.

1973

H247   Anonymous: *"Liebelei" Zu Hans Hollmanns Inszenierung in der Komödie Basel.* In: NZZ, Nr. 108, April 20, 1973, 49. [Cf. review in Aufbau, June 1, 1973, p. 15].

H248   ASPETSBERGER, FRIEDBERT: *Arthur Schnitzlers "Der Weg ins Freie."* In: Sprachkunst, 4, i/ii (1973), 65-80. [Italian translation appeared under the title "Arthur Schnitzler. Verso la liberazione" in: "Il romanzo tedesco del Novecento", ed. C. Magris, C. Cases et. al. Torino: Einaudi, 1973, pp. 47-68].

H249   BAUMANN, GERHART: *Arthur Schnitzler.* In: Handbook of Austrian Literature, ed. Frederick Ungar. New York: Frederick Ungar Publishing Co., 1973, pp. 235-240. [Translated from the German version in: Hermann Kunisch, Handbuch der deutschen Gegenwartsliteratur. München: Nymphenburger Verlagshandlung, 1970, pp. 187-190].
Reviewed by:
H249.1 Bergel, Kurt. In: MAL, 8, iii/iv (1975), 417-419.
H249.2 Theobald, Erika. In: Monatshefte, 67, ii (1975), 190-191.

H250   BERLIN, JEFFREY B.: *Political Criticism in Arthur Schnitzler's "Aphorismen und Betrachtungen."* In: Neophilologus, 57, ii (1973), 173-178.

H251   ——————: *Arthur Schnitzler: A Bibliography. I. Primary Literature: 1965-1972; II. Secondary Literature: 1972; III.*

Additions to First Bibliography; IV. Research in Progress; V. Descriptive Listing of Schnitzler Dissertations: 1917-1972. In: MAL, 6, i/ii (1973), 81-122.

H252 DIERSCH, MANFRED: *Empiriokritizismus und Impressionismus. Über Beziehungen zwischen Philosophie, Ästhetik und Literatur um 1900 in Wien.* Berlin: Rütten & Loening, 1973, 312 p. [Pp. 83-115: Arthur Schnitzler. "Fräulein Else" — literarische Gestaltung impressionistischer Weltsicht im inneren Monolog; pp. 116-127: Schnitzler, Freud und die Psychoanalyse].
Reviewed by:
H252.1 Lindken, Hans-Ulrich. In: MAL, 8, iii/iv (1975), 407-410.
H252.2 Nehring, Wolfgang. In: GQ, 49, ii (1976), 216-217.

H253 ECKERT, WILLEHAD PAUL: *Arthur Schnitzler und das Wiener Judentum.* In: EMUNA. Horizonte zur Discussion über Israel und das Judentum (Frankfurt a.M.), 8, ii (1973), 118-130. [This issue devoted to theme of "Judentum in Wien und Österreich"].

H254 ENDLER, FRANZ: *Österreich zwischen den Zeilen. Die Verwandlung von Land und Volk seit 1848 im Spiegel der "Presse."* Wien: Verlag Fritz Molden, 370 p. [Contains material on "Das süße Mädel"]
Reviewed by:
H254.1 Brude-Firnau, Gisela. In: MAL, 8, iii/iv (1975), 412-414.

H255 GRACE, MATTHEW: *La Ronde.* In: A Reader's Guide to 50 European Plays. New York: Washington Square Press, 1973, pp. 174-185. [Plot outline, with brief evaluation].

H256 GREEN, JON D.: *Musical Structure and Meaning in Arthur Schnitzler's "Zwischenspiel."* In: MAL, 6, i/ii (1973), 7-25.

H257 HAIDA, PETER: *Arthur Schnitzler.* In: P. H., Komödie um 1900. Wandlungen des Gattungsschemas von Hauptmann bis Sternheim. München: Wilhelm Fink Verlag, 1973, pp. 75-91. [Komödie als Thema; Die Karusselstruktur; Die Einakter; Relativierung der Endpositionen].
Reviewed by:
H257.1 Hinze, Klaus-Peter. In: MAL, 8, iii/iv (1975), 426-427.
H257.2 Hryńczuk, Jan. In: Germanistik, 15, iv (1974), 954.

H258 HOEFERT, SIGFRID: *Arthur Schnitzler.* In: Das Drama des Naturalismus. 2nd Edition. Stuttgart: J. B. Metzlersche Verlagsbuchhandlung, 1973, pp. 69-72. [Schnitzler and "Naturalism," with selective bibliography].

H259 HORWATH, PETER: *The Literary Treatment of the French Revolution: A Mirror Reflecting the Changing Nature of Austrian Liberalism (1862-1899).* In: MAL, 6, i/ii (1973). [Pp. 35-36 discuss Schnitzler]

H260   IDEN, PETER: *Schnitzlers "Liebelei." Hart und bitter gegen Wien.* In: Theater heute, 14, vi (1973), 20-22. [Hans Hollmann's production in Basel].

H261   JANIK, ALLAN and STEPHEN TOULMIN: *Wittgenstein's Vienna.* New York: Simon and Schuster, 1973, 314 p. [Schnitzler: pp. 62-63, and passim].
Reviewed by:
H261.1 Klarmann, Adolf. In: BA, 48, ii (1974), 370-371.
H261.2 Winslade, William J. In: MAL, 6, iii/iv (1973), 234-237.

H262   KAISER, JOACHIM: *Hollmanns Intensität: zerstörerisch und produktiv. Neuinszenierung von Schnitzlers "Leibelei" im Basler Theater.* In: Süddeutsche Zeitung, April 21-23, 1973, 35.

H263   KROTKOFF, HERTHA: *Zur geheimen Gesellschaft in Arthur Schnitzlers "Traumnovelle."* In: GQ, 46, ii (1973), 202-209.

H264   MANN, HEINRICH: *Arthur Schnitzler.* In: Heinrich Mann. Ein Zeitalter wird besichtigt. Ed. Deutsche Akademie der Künste zu Berlin. Berlin and Weimar: Aufbau-Verlag, 1973, pp. 234-242. [First in 1947 edition].

H 265   MÖHRMANN, RENATE: *Der vereinsamte Mensch. Studien zum Wandel des Einsamkeitsmotivs von Raabe bis Musil.* Bonn: Bouvier Verlag, 1973. [1972 dissertation. See R.M., "Der Weg ins Freie," in: WW (23, vi [1973], 390-400)].
Reviewed by:
H265.1 Haenicke, Diether H. In: GQ, 49, ii (1976), 210-212.

H266   ––––––: *Impressionistische Einsamkeit bei Schnitzler. Dargestellt an seinem Roman "Der Weg ins Freie."* In: WW, 23, vi (1973), 390-400.

H267   OFFERMANNS, ERNST L.: *Arthur Schnitzler. Das Komödienwerk als Kritik des Impressionismus.* München: Wilhelm Fink Verlag, 1973, 244 p.
Reviewed by:
H267.1 Derré, Françoise. In: EG, 4 (1974), 525-527.
H267.2 Kuttenkeuler, Wolfgang. In: Germanistik, 15 (1974), 467.
H267.3 Schürer, Ernst. In: BA, 49, i (1975), 116.
H267.4 Wonderly, A. Wayne. In: GQ, 40, i (1976), 120.

H268   PASCAL, ROY: *From Naturalism to Expressionism. German Literature and Society 1880-1918.* London: Weidenfeld and Nicolson, 1973.

H269   POS, W.P.: *A Precious Jewel in Schnitzler's 'String' of One-Act Plays.* In: Essays on Drama and Theatre. Presented to Professor Dr. B. Hunningher. Amsterdam: Moussault's Uitgeverij bv, 1973, pp. 129-139.

H270   REICHERT, HERBERT W.: *The Ethical Import of the Artist in the Works of Arthur Schnitzler.* In: MAL, 6, i/ii (1973), 123-150.

H271 REISS, FRANÇOISE: *Thèses en Sorbonne 1963-1969.* Paris: Éditions Klincksieck, 1973. [Pp. 70-74: résumé of Françoise Derré's "L'oeuvre d'Arthur Schnitzler. Imagerie viennoise et problèmes humains."].

H272 RIEDER, HEINZ: *Arthur Schnitzler. Das dramatische Werk.* Wien: Bergland Verlag, 1973, 108 p.
Reviewed by:
H272.1 Derré, Françoise. In: EG, 29, ii (1974), 261-262.
H272.2 Kuttenkeuler, Wolfgang. In: Germanistik, 15, iii (1974), 730.
H272.3 Rey, William H. In: MAL, 7, i/ii (1974), 192-194.
H272.4 Sondrup, Steven P. In: BA, 49, i (1975), 117.

H273 SEGAR, KENNETH: *Determinism and Character: Arthur Schnitzler's "Traumnovelle" and his Unpublished Critique of Psychoanalysis,* In: Oxford German Studies, 8 (1973), 114-127.

H274 SEVIN, DIETER: *Arthur Schnitzlers Gestalt des erotischen Abenteuers.* In: University of Dayton Review, 10, i (1973), 59-65. [Considers "Anatol," "Der einsame Weg" and "Casanovas Heimfahrt."].

H275 TROCKIJ, LEV D.: *Über Arthur Schnitzler.* In: L. D. T., Literaturtheorie und Literaturkritik. Ausgew. Aufsätze zur Literatur. Ed. Ulrich Mölk. Tr. U. M. and Thomas Kunke. München: Wilhelm Fink Verlag, 1973, pp. 62-74. [Translation of 1902 Russian study; cf. review in Germanistik, 14, iv (1973), 762].

H276 URBACH, REINHARD: *Arthur Schnitzler.* Tr. Donald G. Daviau. New York: Frederick Ungar Publishing Co., 1973, 202 p. [Translation of 2nd Edition].
Reviewed by:
H276.1 Alter, Maria P. In: GQ, (September, 1975), 138-139.
H276.2 Beharriell, Frederick J. In: Monatshefte, 67, ii (1975), 212-213.
H276.3 Doswald, Herman K. In: MAL, 7 i/ii (1974), 200-201.
H276.4 Swales, Martin. In: BA, 48, ii (1974), 371.

H277 WEBER, EUGENE: *The Correspondence of Arthur Schnitzler and Richard Beer-Hofmann.* In: MAL, 6, iii/iv (1973), 40-51.

1974

H278 ALEWYN, RICHARD: *Zweimal Liebe: Schnitzlers "Liebelei" und "Reigen."* In: R. A., Probleme und Gestalten. Essays. Frankfurt a.M.: Insel Verlag, 1974, pp. 299-307. [Reprint of "Nachwort" in R. A.'s edition of "Liebelei − Reigen" (Frankfurt a.M.: Fischer Bücherei, 1960].

H279 ALEXANDER, THEODOR W.: *Olga Waissnix: The Model for the Character of the Married Woman in the Early Works of Arthur Schnitzler.* In: MAL, 7, i/ii (1974), 99-107.

H280 BEER, OTTO F.: *Der 42 1/2. Todestag. Wiener Festwochen: Schnitzler auf allen Bühnen.* In: Süddeutsche Zeitung, Nr. 123 (May 29, 1974), 12. [Discusses presentations of "Anatol," "Professor Bernhardi" and "Freiwild."].

H281 BERLIN, JEFFREY B.: *The Element of 'Hope' in Arthur Schnitzler's "Sterben."* In: Seminar. A Journal of Germanic Studies, 10, i (1974), 38-49.

H282 ———————: *Arthur Schnitzler's "Die Frau mit dem Dolche:" Déjà Vu Experience or Hypnotic Trance?* In: MAL, 7, i/ii (1974), 108-112.

H283 ———————: *Arthur Schnitzler Bibliography for 1973-1974.* In: MAL, 7, i/ii (1974), 174-191.

H284 BUBER, MARTIN: *On Viennese Literature.* Tr. Robert A. Rothstein. In: GQ, 47, iv (1974), 559-566. [Translation of Buber's 1897 Polish essay. Schnitzler: pp. 564-566].

H285 DOPPLER, ALFRED: *Das Konversationsstück bei Arthur Schnitzler und Hugo von Hofmannsthal.* In: Sprachthematik in der österreichischen Literatur des 20. Jahrhunderts. Wien: Ferdinand Hirt Verlag, 1974, pp. 69-82.

H286 FRITSCHE, ALFRED: *Dekadenz im Werk Arthur Schnitzlers.* Bern: Herbert Lang, 1974, 278 p.
Reviewed by:
H286.1 Daviau, Donald G. In: MAL, 10, i (1977), 93-95.
H286.2 Derré, Françoise. In: EG, 31, i (1976), 94-95.

H287 GAISBAUER, ADOLF: *Der historische Hintergrund von Arthur Schnitzlers "Professor Bernhardi,"* In: Bulletin des Leo Baeck Instituts, 13, 1 (1974), 113-163

H288 GLASER, HORST: *Arthur Schnitzler und Frank Wedekind − Der doppelköpfige Sexus.* In: Wollüstige Phantasie. Sexualästhetik der Literatur. Ed. H.G. München: Hanser, 1974, pp. 148-184.
Reviewed by:
H288.1 Köpf, Gerhard. In: MAL, iii/iv (1975), 423-426.

H289 GROSSBERG, MIMI: *Arthur Schnitzlers Porträt eines Leutnants.* In: M. G., Die k.u.k. Armee in der österreichischen Satire. Wien: Bergland Verlag, 1974, pp. 31-36.
Reviewed by:
H289.1 Koppensteiner, Jürgen. In: MAL, iii/iv (1975), 414-415.

H290 HAUSER, RONALD: *Georg Büchner.* New York: Twayne Publishers, Inc., 1974. [Pp. 132-133 discuss Schnitzler and Büchner].

H291 JOHNSTON, WILLIAM M.: *Martin Buber's Literary Debut: "On Viennese Literature" (1897).* In: GQ, 47, iv (1974), 556-558. [Discusses Buber's 1897 Polish essay on Bahr, Hofmannsthal, Altenberg and Schnitzler. Translation of essay follows].

H292 *Jugend in Wien. Literatur um 1900.* Eine Ausstellung des Deutschen Literaturarchivs im Schiller-Nationalmuseum Marbach a.N. Ed. Bernhard Zeller. München: Kösel Verlag, 1974, 444 p. [Contains numerous important quotations from critical studies].
Reviewed by:
H292.1 Fischer, Jens Malte. In: Germanistik, 15, iii (1974), 683-684.
H292.2 Frankenstein, Alfred. In: LuK, 94 (1975), 244-245

H293 KANN, ROBERT A.: *A History of the Habsburg Empire 1526-1918.* Berkeley: University of California Press, 1974, 646 p. [More important than the discussion of Schnitzler (pp. 545-546) is the "Bibliographical Essay" (pp. 565-600) that contains references on Schnitzler's period].

H294 KLUGE, GERHARD: *Die Dialektik von Illusion und Erkenntnis als Strukturprinzip des Einakters bei Arthur Schnitzler.* In: Jahrbuch der deutschen Schillergesellschaft, 18 (1974), 482-505.

H295 LAWSON, RICHARD H.: *Edith Wharton and German Literature.* Bonn: Bouvier Verlag, 1974. [Pp. 46-50: "Das süße Mädel" in Schnitzler's and Wharton's work].

H296 LERNET-HOLENIA, ALEXANDER: *Arthur Schnitzler.* In: Programmheft des Theaters in der Josefstadt (1974/75), 6-8. [Reprinted from Frankfurter Allgemeine Zeitung (May 15, 1972)].

H297 LOW, D.S.: *Schnitzler's "Sterben." A Technique of Narrative Perspective.* In: Festschrift for C. P. Magill. Ed. H. Siefken and A. Robinson. Cardiff: University of Wales Press, 1974, pp. 126-135.

H298 MAYER, HANS: *Obszönität und Pornographie in Film und Theater.* In: Akzente, 21, iv (1974), 372-383. [Discusses "Reigen."].

H299 NEHRING, WOLFGANG: *Hofmannsthal und der österreichische Impressionismus.* In: Hofmannsthal-Forschungen II. Referate und Diskussionen der dritten Tagung der Hugo von Hofmannsthal-Gesellschaft. Freiburg i. Br., 1974. [Pp. 62-63: Schnitzler's impressionistik works.]

H300 POLITZER, HEINZ: *Die letzten Tage der Schwierigen. Hofmannsthal, Karl Kraus und Schnitzler.* In: Merkur, 28, iii (1974), 214-238.

H301 SCHINNERER, OTTO P.: *Introduction.* In: Arthur Schnitzler, Viennese Novelettes. New York: AMS Press, Inc., 1974, pp. vii-xlv. [Reprinted from 1931 Simon & Schuster edition.]

H302 SPIEL, HILDE: *Das Wienerische und das Schnitzlerische. "Freiwild," "Anatol," und "Professor Bernhardi" auf Wiener Bühnen.* In: Theater heute, 15, vii (1974), 13-15.

H303 STEWART, DESMOND: *Theodor Herzl.* Garden City: Doubleday & Co., Inc. 1974. [Pp. 61-62, 141, 146-147, 152-154 & 162-163: Schnitzler's and Herzl's relationship and Schnitzler as a critic of Herzl's "The New Ghetto].

H304   URBACH, REINHARD: *Schnitzler Kommentar zu den erzählenden Schriften und dramatischen Werken.* München: Winkler Verlag, 1974, 210 p. [Bibliographical material, explications of textual allusions, phrases, words and references, notes on and publication of textual variants or early drafts from the "Nachlaß," significant letters, material from the diaries.].
Reviewed by:
H304.1 Berlin, Jeffrey B. In: Germano-Slavica. A Canadian journal of Germanic and Slavic comparative studies, 2, i (1976), 66-69.
H304.2 Daviau, Donald G. In: MAL, 8, iii/iv (1975), 360-362.
H304.3 Derré, Françoise. In: EG, 30, iii (1975), 365-366.
H304.4 Koch, Hans-Albrecht. In: Germanistik, 16, ii (1975), 554.
H304.5 Offermanns, Ernst L. In: ZDP, 95, ii (1976), 308-310.
H304.6 Schlein, Rena R. In: Monatshefte, 68, i (1976), 102-103.
H304.7 Swales, Martin. In: BA, 49, ii (1975), 322.

H305   –––––––: *Aktion und Passion in Arthur Schnitzlers "Puppenspieler."* In: Programmheft des Theaters in der Josefstadt (1974/75), 2-5.

H306   –––––––: *"Reigen" in Syracuse. Arthur Schnitzler in der amerikanischen Provinz.* In: NZZ, Nr. 500 (Nov. 25, 1974), 17. [Theater review of "Reigen" (under direction of Arthur Storch). Contains noteworthy information].

H307   –––––––: *Arthur Schnitzler.* In: Tausend Jahre Österreich. Ed. Walter Pollak. Bd. 3. Wien: Jugend und Volk, 1974, pp. 104-109. [Brief sketch of major ideas in Schnitzler's works].

H308   –––––––: *Crêpe de Chine. Karl Kraus und die Zeitschrift "Liebelei."* In: NZZ, Nr. 194, April 28, 1974, 52.

H309   URBAN, BERND: *Arthur Schnitzler und Sigmund Freud. Aus den Anfängen des "Doppelgängers." Zur Differenzierung dichterischer Intuition und Umgebung der frühen Hysterieforschung.* In: Germanisch-Romanische Monatsschrift, 24, ii (1974), 193-223.

H310   WAGNER, RENATE: *Der Dichter und die Schauspielerin: Arthur Schnitzler und Adele Sandrock.* In: NZZ, Nr. 297 (June 30, 1974), 53.

H311   –––––––: *Arthur Schnitzler liebt Adele Sandrock. Dichter und Schauspielerin im Wiener Fin de siècle.* In: Theater heute, 15, ix (Sept., 1974), 28-30. [Additional information on the Schnitzler-Sandrock relationship].

H312   WERBA, ROBERT: *Ein Außenseiter der Theaterkritik. Peter Altenberg und das Wiener Theaterjahr 1898/99.* In: Maske und Kothurn, 20, ii (1974), 163-190. [Pp. 166-167: reprint of Altenberg's feuilleton of Dec. 5, 1898 (in "Wiener 'Extrapost' ") concerning Schnitzler's "Das Vermächtnis" (in Burgtheater, Nov. 30,

1898); pp. 167-168: commentary by Werba; pp. 176-178: reprint of Altenberg's feuilleton of March 6, 1899 (in "Wiener 'Extrapost' ") concerning Schnitzler's "Paracelsus," "Die Gefährtin" and "Der grüne Kakadu" (in Burgtheater March 1, 1899); pp. 178-179: commentary by Werba].

H313   WILLENBERG, HEINER: *Die Darstellung des Bewußtseins in der Literatur. Vergleichende Studien zu Philosophie, Psychologie und deutscher Literatur von Schnitzler bis Broch.* Frankfurt a.M.: Akademische Verlagsgesellschaft, 1974, 169 p. [Pp. 75-95: "Leutnant Gustl" and "Fräulein Else"].

H314   WILLIAMS, C. E.: *The Broken Eagle. The Politics of Austrian Literature from Empire to Anschluss.* New York: Barnes and Noble, 1974, 281 p. [Chapter 3 (pp. 45-59): Arthur Schnitzler. The Astigmatic Vision].
Reviewed by:
H314.1 Schwarz, Egon. In: GQ, 49, iv (1976), 502-504.
H314.2 Swales, Martin. In: MLR, 71, iv (1976), 971-973.

H315   WISTRICH, ROBERT: *Arthur Schnitzler's "Jewish Problem."* In: The Jewish Quarterly, 22, iii (82), 1974/75, 27-30.

1975

H316   BAUMANN, GERHART: *Arthur Schnitzlers Tagebücher. Eine Welt in Tagen – Jahrzehnte einer Welt.* In: NZZ, Nr. 230, October 4/5, 1975, 59.

H317   BERLIN, JEFFREY B.: *Arthur Schnitzler Bibliography for 1974-1975.* In: MAL, 8, iii/iv (1975), 248-265.

H318   *Bibliographisches Handbuch der deutschen Literatur: 1945-1972.* Bd. 2, Lieferung 11, ed. Clemens Köttelwesch. Frankfurt a.M.: Vittorio Klostermann, 1975. [Schnitzler: pp. 871-884. Contains bibliographical material. However, all is already recorded in the Allen and Berlin bibliographies. Very useful for related authors at turn-of-the-century].

H319   BLACKALL, ERIC A.: *Tobias Klenk* [in: Die Frau des Richters]. In: Austriaca. Beiträge zur österreichischen Literatur. Festschrift für Heinz Politzer zum 65. Geburtstag. Ed. Richard Brinkmann, Winfried Kudszus and Hinrich Seeba. Tübingen: Max Niemeyer Verlag, 1975, pp. 267-284.
Reviewed by:
H319.1 Hoover, Marjorie L. In: BA, 50, iv (1976), 521.

H320   COOK, WILLIAM K.: *Isolation, Flight, and Resolution in Arthur Schnitzler's "Die Toten schweigen."* In: GR, 50, iii (1975), 213-226.

H321   DOPPLER, ALFRED: *Die Form des Einakters und die Spielmetapher bei Arthur Schnitzler.* In: Alfred Doppler,

Wirklichkeit im Spiegel der Sprache. Aufsätze zur Literatur des 20. Jahrhunderts in Österreich. Wien: Europa Verlag, 1975, pp. 7-30.

H322 ——————: *Die Problematik der Sprache und des Sprechens in den Bühnenstücken Arthur Schnitzlers.* In: Alfred Doppler, Wirklichkeit im Spiegel der Sprache. Aufsätze zur Literatur des 20. Jahrhunderts in Österreich. Wien: Europa Verlag, 1975, pp. 31-52.

H323 ——————: *Innerer Monolog und soziale Wirklichkeit. Arthur Schnitzlers Novelle "Leutnant Gustl."* In: Alfred Doppler, Wirklichkeit im Spiegel der Sprache. Aufsätze zur Literatur des 20. Jahrhunderts in Österreich. Wien: Europa Verlag, 1975, pp. 53-64.

H324 ELON, AMOS: *Herzl.* New York: Holt, Reinehart and Winston, 1975. [See esp. pp. 47-48, 109-111 and 124-126].

H325 GROSSBERG, MIMI: *Schnitzleriade (1975).* In: Aufbau (April 4, 1975), p. 40. [Poem modeled after Hugo von Hofmannsthal's introduction to "Anatol"].

H326 HERMAN, WILLIAM and DENNIS DE NITTO: *Film and the Critical Eye.* New York: Macmillan Publishing Co., 1975, 543 p. [Pp. 272-289: Ophuls' "La Ronde"].

H327 KATHREIN, KARIN: *Schnitzler: Welt in Tagebüchern. 5000 Seiten warten auf Entdeckung.* In: Die Presse (Wien), Dec. 24, 1975, 7.

H328 LAWSON, RICHARD H. and PEGGY STAMON: *Love-Death Structures in the Works of Arthur Schnitzler.* In: MAL, 8, iii/iv (1975), 266-281.

H329 MOMOS [= Walter Jens]: *Sudermann im Wiener Dialekt.* In: Die Zeit, Nr. 41, Oct. 3, 1975, 42. [Review of "Komtesse Mizzi" television production].

H330 NENNECKE, CHARLOTTE: *Fünf Abenteuer eines Wiener Charmeurs. Arthur Schnitzlers "Anatol" im Residenztheater.* In: Süddeutsche Zeitung, Nr. 30 (Feb. 6, 1975), 13. [Theater review of "Anatol" (under direction of Kurt Meisel) in Munich's Residenztheater].

H331 REICHERT, HERBERT W.: *Nietzsche's "Geniemoral" and Schnitzler's Ethics.* In: H. W. R., Friedrich Nietzsche's Impact on Modern German Literature. Five Essays. Chapel Hill: University of North Carolina Press, 1975, pp. 4-28.

H332 SCHLEIN, RENA: *Das Duellmotive in Schnitzlers Dramen "Ritterlichkeit," "Das weite Land" und "Das Wort."* In: MAL, 8, iii/iv (1975), 222-235.

H333 SELLING, GUNTER: *Die Einakter und Einakterzyklen Arthur Schnitzlers.* Amsterdam: Editions Rodopi, 1975, 246 p.
Reviewed by:
H333.1 Derré, Françoise. In: Germanistik, 17, i (1976), 349-350.
H333.2 Swales, Martin. In: BA, 50, iii (1976), 656.

H334   SKASA, MICHAEL: *Weder Pfau noch Bologneserhündchen. Kurt Meisel inszenierte Schnitzlers "Anatol" am Münchner Residenztheater.* In: Süddeutsche Zeitung (Feb. 8/9, 1975).

H335   SWALES, MARTIN: *Nürnberger's Novel: A Study of Arthur Schnitzler's "Der Weg ins Freie."* In: MLR, 70, iii (1975), 567-575.

H336   URBACH, REINHARD: *Arthur Schnitzler: "Das Vermächtnis."* In: Programmheft des Theaters in der Josefstadt (1975/76), 3-6.

H337   –––––––: *Leibhaftiges Dilemma der Jahrhundertwende. Bemerkungen zu Richard Schaukal.* In: NZZ, Nr. 96, April 26/27, 1975, 57-58. [Schnitzler und Schaukal].

H338   –––––––: *Karl Kraus und die Nachwelt. Beschäftigung mit dem Wiener Schriftsteller hundert Jahre nach seiner Geburt.* In: NZZ, Nr. 129, June 7/8, 1975, 61-62. [Reference to Schnitzler].

H339   URNER, HANS: *Schnitzlers Paracelsus.* In: Paracelsus. Werk und Wirkung. Festgabe für Kurt Goldammer zum 60. Geburtstag. Hrsg. Sepp Domandl. Wien: Verlag Verband der wissenschaftlichen Österreichs, 1975, pp. 345-352.

                                    1976

H340   ALTHAUS, HORST: *Zwischen Monarchie und Republik. Schnitzler-Hofmannsthal-Kraus-Musil.* München: Wilhelm Fink Verlag, 1976, 188 p. [Schnitzler, pp. 39-79].

H341   BÄUML, GUSTAV H. und FRANZ H. BÄUML: *Namenverzeichnis zu Karl Kraus' "Die Fackel".* In: MAL, 9, i (1976). [Schnitzler, pp. 65-66].

H342   BERLIN, JEFFREY B.: *A Survey of Scholarship on Schnitzler: 1965-1975.* In: J.B.B. The Treatment of Truth in the Dramatic Work of Henrik Ibsen and Arthur Schnitzler. Ph.D. diss. State University of New York at Binghamton, 1976, Appendix B, pp. 473-596. [Year by year summarization of the majority of critical studies on Schnitzler for the period 1965-1975. Completely different from Seidler's (see item 353) "Forschungsbericht." However, his valuable work is of major importance and can well be used in conjunction with the above analyses].

H343   –––––––: *Arthur Schnitzler Bibliography for 1975-1976.* In: MAL, 9, ii (1976), 63-72. [Includes photos of Schnitzler works and Schnitzler from J. Berlin collection].

H344   GARLAND, MARY and HENRY: *"Arthur Schnitzler."* In: Mary and Henry Garland, The Oxford Companion to German Literature. Oxford: The Clarendon Press, 1976, pp. 771-772. [Brief sketch of Schnitzler's life and work].

H345   *Hätte ich das Kino! Die Schriftsteller und der Stummfilm.* Eine Ausstellung des Deutschen Literaturarchivs im Schiller-Nationalmuseum Marbach a.N. Ed. Bernhard Zeller. München: Kösel Verlag, 1976, 444 p. [See esp. pp. 147-150 and 198-205].

H346   *Das Junge Wien. Österreichische Literatur- und Kunstkritik 1887-1902.* Ed. Gotthart Wunberg. Tübingen: Max Niemeyer Verlag, 1976. 2 Bde. 1347 p. [Invaluable reference work].

H347   KROTKOFF, HERTHA H.: *Ein Artikel von A.S..* In: MAL, 9, ii (1976), 55-62. [Demonstrates that an article written about T. Mann and signed A.S. was not Arthur Schnitzler].

H348   LEROY, ROBERT and ECKART PASTOR: *Der Sprung ins Bewußtsein. Zu einigen Erzählungen von Arthur Schnitzler.* In: ZDP, 95, iv (1976), 481-495.

H349   PRANG, HELMUT: *Arthur Schnitzlers Regieanweisungen.* In: Grillparzer Jahrbuch, 12, (1976), 257-275.

H350   SCHEIBLE, HARTMUT: *Arthur Schnitzler in Selbstzeugnissen und Bilddokumenten.* Reinbek bei Hamburg: Rowohlt Taschenbuch Verlag GmbH, 1976, 157 p.
Reviewed by:
H350.1 Urbach, Reinhard. In: NZZ, (Jan. 8/9, 1977), Nr. 6, 50.

H351   ————: *"Nachwort."* In: Arthur Schnitzler. "Die Braut." "Traumnovelle." Ed. Hartmut Scheible. Stuttgart: Philipp Reclam Jun., 1976, pp. 105-127.

H352   SCHWARZ, EGON: *Schnitzlers vielschichtige Wahrheit. Eine Interpretation von "Komtesse Mizzi oder Der Familientag".* In: Herkommen und Erneuerung. Essays für Oskar Seidlin, ed. Gerald Gillespie and Edgar Lohner. Tübingen: Max Niemeyer Verlag, 1976, pp. 268-281.

H353   SEIDLER, HERBERT: *Die Forschung zu Arthur Schnitzler seit 1945.* In: ZDP, 95, iv (1976), 567-595. [cf. item H342].

H354   SPIEL, HILDE: *"Nachwort."* In: Arthur Schnitzler, "Traumnovelle." Ed. Hilde Spiel. Frankfurt a.M.: S. Fischer, 1976, pp. 140-151.

H355   URBACH, REINHARD: *Arthur Schnitzlers letztes Werk* [Im Spiel der Sommerlüfte]. In: Programmheft des Theaters in der Josefstadt, Spielzeit 1976/77 (Premiere October 7, 1976), pp. 8-10.

H356   WEISS, ROBERT O.: *Schnitzler's Ideas on "Schmutzliteratur" and the Marriage Contract.* In: MAL, 9, ii (1976), 50-54.

I. Dissertations

1965

I1   DERRÉ, FRANÇOISE: *L'oeuvre d'Arthur Schnitzler. Imagerie viennoise et problémes humains.* 600 p. Sorbonne. [Published, Paris: Marcel Didier, 1966. See secondary literatures listing for reviews].

I2   JUST, GOTTFRIED: *Ironie und Sentimentalität in den erzählenden Dichtung Arthur Schnitzlers.* 149 p. Tübingen. [Published, Berlin: Erich Schmidt Verlag, 1968. See secondary literature listing for reviews].

I3   KUXDORF, MANFRED: *Das Schicksal im Werk Arthur Schnitzlers*, 128 p. M. A., University of Waterloo.

I4   WILEY, MARION E.: *The "Einakter" as Dance of Wit ("Spiel") and Court of Justice ("Gericht"): A Structural Analysis of German One-Act Plays from Goethe to Dürrenmatt.* 260 p. Pennsylvania State University. Summary in: DA, XXVI, xi (1965), 6728.

1966

I5   NARDROFF, ERNEST HENRY VON: *Aspects of Symbolism in the Works of Arthur Schnitzler.* 251 p. Columbia University. Summary in: DA, XXVII, vi A (1966), 1842 A.

I6   TYLER, DONALD H.: *"Das süsse Mädel" in the Works of Arthur Schnitzler.* 89 p. M.A. Thesis San Diego State University.

I7   VACHA, BRIGITTE: *Arthur Schnitzler und das Wiener Burgtheater 1895-1965.* 341 p. Wien. Shortened version published as "Wiener Schnitzler-Aufführungen 1891-1970," (co-author: Renate Wagner). München: Prestel-Verlag, 1971. [See secondary literature listing for reviews].

I8   WALTON, SARAH LUVERNE: *Arthur Schnitzler on the New York Stage.* 204 p. Indiana University. Summary in: DA, XXVII, xii A (1966), 4269-70 A.

1967

I9   KLEIN, L.C.: *The Portrait of the Jew in English and German Fiction and Drama (1830-1933).* University College, London. [Schnitzler: pp. 264-265].

I10   MELCHINGER, CHRISTA: *Illusion und Wirklichkeit im dramatischen Werk Arthur Schnitzlers.* 138 p. Hamburg. [Published, Heidelberg: Carl Winter, 1968. See secondary literature listing for reviews].

I11   SCHLEIN, RENA R.: *The Treatment of Hypocrisy in the Works of Arthur Schnitzler.* 65 p. M. A., New York University. [Shortened version published as "The Motif of Hypocrisy in the Works of Arthur Schnitzler," MAL, II, i (1969), 28-38.].

I12   WHITON, JOHN N.: *The Problem of Marriage in the Works of Arthur Schnitzler.* 277 p. University of Minnesota. Summary in: DA, XXVIII, vii A (1967), 2701 A.

1968

I13   GORLIN, LALLA: *The Problem of Loneliness in the Works of Arthur Schnitzler.* 265 p. Columbia University. Summary in: DA, XXXII, iii (1971), 1511 A.

I14   NOLTENIUS, RAINER: *Hofmannsthal – Schröder – Schnitzler: Möglichkeiten und Grenzen des modernen Aphorismus.* 256 p. Mainz. [Published, Stuttgart: J. B. Metzlersche Verlagsbuchhandlung, 1969. (Schnitzler: pp. 141-199. See secondary literature listing for reviews].

I15   SCHNEIDER, GERD KLAUS: *Arthur Schnitzler und die Psychologie seiner Zeit, unter besonderer Berücksichtigung der Philosophie Friedrich Nietzsches.* 389 p. University of Washington. Summary in: DA, XXIX, vii A (1968), 2281-82 A.

I16   SZEKELY, GABRIELLA MARIA: *The Role of Temporal Continuity in Arthur Schnitzler's Dramatic Works.* 72 p. M.A., State University of New York at Binghamton.

I17   WILLIAMS, CEDRIC ELLIS: *Austrian Politics and Literature, 1914-1938: The Impact of the First World War and its Aftermath upon Austrian Literature.* 271 p. Cambridge. [Schnitzler: pp. 87-98. Published in 1974. See secondary literature listing for reviews].

I18   YU, CHONG-KU: *Spiel und Spielertum in den Komödien Arthur Schnitzlers.* 104 p. Mag. – Arb., München.

1969

I19   GROTE, MARIE: *Themes and Variations in the Early Prose Fiction of Arthur Schnitzler* 72 p. M.A., Duke University. Published, MAL, III, iv (1970), 22-47.

I20   HOPP, GERALD G.: *A Comparison of Motifs and Attitudes in the Works of Schnitzler and Chekhov.* 85 p. M.A., University of Pittsburgh.

I21   IMBODEN, MICHAEL: *Die surreale Komponente im erzählenden Werk Arthur Schnitzlers.* 131 p. Freiburg. [Published, Bern: Herbert Lang Verlag, 1971. See secondary literature listing for reviews].

I22   KHATIB, ADEL: *Casanovas Wiederkehr: Seine Gestalt im Werk Hofmannsthals und Schnitzlers.* 88 p. Mag. – Arb., München.

I23   KILIAN, KLAUS: *Die Komödien Arthur Schnitzlers. Sozialer Rollenzwang und kritische Ethik.* Bochum. [Published, Düsseldorf: Bertelsmann Universitätsverlag, 1972, 179 p. See secondary literature listing for reviews].

I24   REID, MARIA DORA H.: *Aspects of Theme and Technique in Arthur Schnitzler's Shorter Prose Fiction.* 218 p. University of California, Los Angeles. Summary in: DA, XXX, viii A (1970), 3473-3474 A.

I25   TÖRÖK, ANDREW: *Der Widerspruch zwischen Gefühl und Verstand bei Arthur Schnitzler.* 164 p. University of Minnesota.

I26   WAGNER, RENATE: *Wiener Schnitzler-Aufführungen 1891-1968 (bei Otto Brahms Gastspielen in Wien, im Volkstheater und im*

Theater in der Josefstadt). 426 p. Wien. [Shortened version published as "Wiener Schnitzler-Aufführungen 1891-1970," (co-author: Brigitte Vacha). München: Prestel-Verlag, 1971. See secondary literature listing for reviews].

I27 WEIßBERG-DRONIA, MIRA: *Selbstverständnis und Welterfahrung in Arthur Schnitzlers frühen Dramen*. 170 p. Freiburg im Breisgau.

1970

I28 DRIVER, BEVERLEY ROSE: *Herman Bang and Arthur Schnitzler: Modes of the Impressionist Narrative*. 228 p. Indiana University. Summary in: DA, XXXI, vii A (1970), 3543 A.

I29 GRAVES, WILLIAM ROBERT: *The Development of Arthur Schnitzler's Narrative Technique: 1885-1900*. 78 p. M.A., State University of New York at Binghamton.

I30 LEBENSAFT, ELIZABETH: *Anordnung und Funktion zentraler Aufbauelemente in den Erzählungen Arthur Schnitzlers*. 184 p. Wien. [Published. See secondary literature for reviews].

I31 ROTH, HEIDEMARIE: *Der Einakter um die Jahrhundertwende und seine literaturgeschichtlichen Voraussetzungen*. 155 p. Wien.

I32 SCHOLZ, GERDA: *Bewusstsein und Wirklichkeit. Zur spätzeitlichen Figur im Werk Arthur Schnitzlers*. 255 p. Freiburg im Breisgau.

I33 SUBOCZEWSKI, IRENE: *The Figure of the Artist in Modern Drama from Ibsen to Pirandello*. University of Maryland, 322 p. Summary in: DA, 31, xi (1970), 6074 A. [Chapter 4 (pp. 145-170): "Lebendige Stunden," "Die Frau mit dem Dolche," "Die letzten Masken," and "Literatur"].

I34 YARNES, GEORGE ERNEST: *Suicide in the Narrative Works of Arthur Schnitzler*. 45 p. M.A., State University of New York at Binghamton.

1971

I35 BARNEY, RICHARD JOHNSTON: *The Evolution of Self: The Concept of Death in the Works of Arthur Schnitzler*. 181 p. Princeton University. Summary in: DA, XXXII, vii (1972), 3987 A.

I36 BERLIN, JEFFREY BENNETT: *Arthur Schnitzler's Attitude Toward Betrayal and Deception*. 193 p. M.A., Temple University. Summary in: Masters Abstracts, IX, iii (1971), 145.

I37 BROST, JULIANE: *Die Frau in den späten Erzählungen Arthur Schnitzlers*. 115 p. Mag. – Arb., München.

I38 EGER, BARBARA FRAME: *Supernatural and Apparently Supernatural Elements in the Works of Arthur Schnitzler*. 257 p. Indiana University. Summary in: DA, XXXII, v A (1971), 2682 A.

I39 LINDKEN, HANS ULRICH: *Erzählweise und Motive der Spätnovellen Arthur Schnitzlers. Dargestellt an Interpretationen einzelner Novellen.* 198 p. Salzburg. [Brief summary in: Sprachkunst, 4, i/ii (1973), 145].

140   MENKE, MARGARETE: *Literatur- und sozialgeschichtliche Studien zu Arthur Schnitzlers Dramen.* 81 p. Mag. – Arb., München.

141   ROSENBAUM, UWE: *Die Gestalt des Schauspielers auf dem deutschen Theater des 19. Jahrhunderts mit der besonderen Berücksichtung der dramatischen Werke von Hermann Bahr, Arthur Schnitzler und Heinrich Mann.* 275 p. Köln.

142   SEGAR, KENNETH: *Psychological determinism and moral responsibility in some narrative works of Arthur Schnitzler.* 277 p. University of Oxford.

143   SPYCHER, PETER: *Gestaltungsprobleme in der Novellistik Arthur Schnitzlers.* 115 p. Zürich.

1972

144   COOK, WILLIAM K.: *Isolation and Communion in Arthur Schnitzler's Early Short Stories.* 192 p. University of Washington. Summary in: DA, XXXIII, xii (1973), 6904 A.

145   GREEN, JON D.: *The Impact of Musical Theme and Structure on the Meaning and Dramatic Unity of Selected Works by Arthur Schnitzler.* 186 p. Syracuse University. Summary in: DA, XXXIII, i (1972), 312 A.

146   MÖHRMANN, RENATE: *Der vereinsamte Mensch. Studien zum Wandel des Einsamkeitsmotivs im Roman von Rabbe bis Musil.* The City University of New York, 302 p. Summary in: DA, XXXIII, iii (1972), 1175 A. [One chapter devoted to "Der Weg ins Freie;" cf. R.M.'s 1973 Wirkendes Wort article].

147   SANDERS, MARTHA R.: *Arthur Schnitzlers Typologie der Charaktergestalten in "Anatol," "Der grüne Kakadu," "Der Schleier der Beatrice," und "Professor Bernhardi."* 114 p. B.A. Honors Thesis, University of Adelaide.

148   SCHLEIN, RENA R.: *Schnitzlers unveröffentlichte Ritterlichkeit-Fragmente und ihre Bedeutung für "Das weite Land" und "Das Wort."* 199 p. The City University of New York. Summary in: DA, XXXIII, ix (1973), 5198 A. [Published. See primary listing for reviews].

149   TUSSING, MARJORIE O.: *The Function of the Symbol in the Modern German Kurzgeschichte.* University of Southern California, 259 p. Summary in: DA, XXXII, vii (1972), 4027 A. [Pp. 127-133 "Blumen;" pp. 166-176 "Leutnant Gustl:" deals with the symbol as a narrative device].

1973

I50   BOWRING, R. J.,: *A Study of the Works of Mori Ōgai.* Ph.D. Diss. Cambridge University, 1973. [M. Ō. [1862-1922]: translator of some Schnitzler works into Japanese; see esp. pp. 197ff.].

I51   CONNER, MAURICE W.: *An Investigation of Three Themes Pertaining to Life and Death in the Works of Arthur Schnitzler, with Particular Emphasis on the Drama "Der Ruf des Lebens."* 170 p. University of Nebraska at Lincoln. Summary in: DA, XXXIV, vii (1974), 4250 A.

I52   EKFELT, NILS: *The Narration of Dreams in the Prose Works of Thomas Mann and Arthur Schnitzler. A Stylistic Study.* 342 p. Indiana University. Summary in: DA, XXXIV, x (1974), 6637 A.

I53   FRITSCHE, ALFRED: *Dekadenz im Werk Arthur Schnitzlers.* 278 p. Universität Bern. [Published, Bern: Herbert Lang Verlag, 1974. See secondary literature for reviews].

I54   HEINDL, BRIGITTA: *Die Gestalt des Arztes im Drama Arthur Schnitzlers und Karl Schönherrs.* 275 p. Universität Wien.

I55   HERRIG, RUDOLF: *Die erzählenden Schriften Arthur Schnitzlers: Erzählsituation, Problemstruktur und Leseerlebnis.* 220 p. University of Pittsburgh. Summary in: DA, XXXV, ii (1974), 1102 A.

I56   SCHMIDT, WILLA: *The Changing Role of Women in the Works of Arthur Schnitzler.* 347 p. University of Wisconsin. Summary in: DA, XXXV, i (1974), 474 A.

I57   SCHWABE, HILKE: *Arthur Schnitzlers "Kurzgeschichten."* 115 p. Mag. − Arb., München.

I58   STARRELS, CAROL S.: *The Problem of the "Puppenspieler" in the Works of Arthur Schnitzler.* 252 p. University of Pennsylvania. Summary in: DA, XXXIV, iv (1973), 1938 A.

I59   WITT, IRMTRAUT: *Jugendstilelemente bei Arthur Schnitzler − unter besonderer Berücksichtigung des Frühwerks.* 113 p. Mag. − Arb., München.

I60   ZENKE, JÜRGEN: *Die deutsche Monologerzählung im 20. Jahrhundert.* 174 p. Köln. [Published, Köln und Wien: Böhlau Verlag, 1976, 174 p. Pp. 57-68: "Fräulein Else:" Die Monologerzählung und die Gattungsproblematik der Novelle; pp. 69-84: "Leutnant Gustl:" Verfehlte Selbstfindung als Satire.].

1974

I61   AYRES, GABRIELLA SZEKELY: *The Theme of Transition in Arthur Schnitzler's Social and Historical Dramas.* 165 p. Tulane University. Summary in: DA, XXXV, iii (1974), 1647 A.

I62   KÖPF, GERHARD: *Skepsis und Verantwortlichkeit. Studien zu Arthur Schnitzlers Tragikomödie "Das Wort."* 508 p. München. [Publication forthcoming, Herbert Lang & Cie. Shortened version published, München: W. & I. M. Salzer, 1976].

163   LEVY, ELIZABETH J.: *The Concept of Jealousy in Selected Works of Arthur Schnitzler.* 111 p. M.A., Temple University. Summary in: Masters Abstracts, XII, iii (1974), 272.

164   MEEKER-EDER, RUTH: *Die historischen Dramen Arthur Schnitzlers.* 73 p. Mag. – Arb., München.

165   TOMLINSON, JOHN G., JR.: *Literature and Social Class in Austria, 1890-1930: Social Meanings in the Lives and Literature of Arthur Schnitzler, Hugo von Hofmannsthal, and Robert Musil.* 201 p. University of Southern California. Summary in: DA, XXXV, vi (1974), 3660-3661 A.

1975

166   GUTT, BARBARA: *Die Emanzipation der Frau bei Arthur Schnitzler.* Freie Universität Berlin. [Volker & Spiess Verlag, 1977].

167   ROSE, INGRID: *Social Stereotypes and Female Actualities: A Dimension of the Social Criticism in Selected Works by Fontane, Hauptmann, Wedekind, and Schnitzler.* Princeton University. Summary in: DA, XXXVII, i (1976), 40 A, [Schnitzler, pp. 206-268].

168   SCHEUZGER, JÜRG: *Das Spiel mit Typen und Typenkonstellationen in den Dramen Arthur Schnitzlers.* 307 p. Zürich. [Published: Juris Druck + Verlag Zürich, 1975].

169   SLAVENAS, MARY G.: *The Figure of the Aesthete in German Literature from 1890 to 1910.* State University of New York at Buffalo (1975), 259 p. Summary in: DA, XXXVI, vii (1976), p. 4528 A. [Schnitzler's "Anatol:" pp. 64-83].

170   STAMON, PEGGY: *New Translations of Three Arthur Schnitzler Stories.* 132 p. M.A. Thesis, San Diego State University.

1976

171   BERLIN, JEFFREY B.: *The Treatment of Truth in the Dramatic Work of Henrik Ibsen and Arthur Schnitzler.* 603 p. State University of New York at Binghamton. Summary in: DA, XXXVII, iii (1976), 1576 A.

172   DENEVE, ALBERT: *Emblem of the Human Spirit: Arthur Schnitzler's "Der Geist im Wort und der Geist in der Tat."* 347 p. State University of New York at Binghamton. Summary in: DA, XXXVI, xii (1976), 8084 A.

1977

173   MORSE, MARGARET: *The Works of Arthur Schnitzler as an Index of Cultural Change: Relationships between the Sexes in Social Reality, Ideology and The Imagination.* University of California at Berkeley, Summary in: DA (1977).

Addendum

ALDEN, MARTHA B.: *Casanova in German Literature.* Ph.D. diss. 1974, University of Virginia, 237 p. Summary in: DA, XXXV, iii (1974), 2257 A. (Schnitzler included).

ALEXANDER, THEODOR W.: *Arthur Schnitzler's Use of Mirrors.* In: Seminar, 14, iii (1978).

DUHAMEL, ROLAND: *Schnitzler und Nietzsche.* In: Amsterdamer Beiträge zur neueren Germanistik, 4, 1-25.

KANZER, MARK: *Freud and His Literary Doubles.* In: American Imago, 33, iii (1976), 231-243.

MINOR, NATA: *Capitales de non-lieu: Vienne, Freud, Schnitzler.* In: Critique, 31, 339-340 (1975), 837-845.

OFFERMANNS, ERNST L.: *Schnitzlers Dramatik.* In: Walter Hinck, ed., Handbuch des deutschen Dramas, BD. 2 Düsseldorf: August Bagel, 1978.

1977

BAUMANN, GERHART: *Arthur Schnitzler: Die Tagebücher.* In: MAL, 10, iii/iv (1977).

BEHARRIELL, FREDERICK J.: *Schnitzler's "Fräulein Else:" Reality and Invention.* In: MAL, 10, iii/iv (1977).

BERLIN, JEFFREY B.: *Politics, Religion and Truth: The Priest Figure in Schnitzler's "Professor Bernhardi."* In: MAL, 10, iii/iv (1977).

DERRÉ, FRANÇOISE: *"Der Weg ins Freie," eine wienerische Schule des Gefühls?* In: MAL, 10, iii/iv (1977).

GOLDSMITH, ULRICH K.: *Der Briefwechsel Fritz von Unruhs mit Arthur Schnitzler.* In: MAL, 10, iii/iv (1977).

HERESCH, ELIZABETH: *Arthur Schnitzler in Russland.* In: MAL, 10, iii/iv (1977).

JANZ, ROLF-PETER and KLAUS LAERMANN: *Arthur Schnitzler. Zur Diagnose des Wiener Bürgertums im Fin de sièle.* Stuttgart: Metzler Verlag, 1977.

KROTKOFF, HERTHA: *Schnitzlers Titelgestaltung. Eine quantitive Analyse.* In: MAL, 10, iii/iv (1977).

MORSE, MARGARET: *Decadence and Social Change. Arthur Schnitzler's Works as an Ongoing Process of Deconstruction.* In: MAL, 10, ii (1977).

NEHRING, WOLFGANG: *Schnitzler, Freud's Alter Ego?* In: MAL, 10, iii/iv (1977).

REY, WILLIAM H.: *"Werden, was ich werden sollte:" Arthur Schnitzlers Jugend als Prozess der Selbstverwirklichung.* In: MAL, 10, iii/iv, (1977).

——————: *Judith – Aurelie – Seraphine. Zu Schnitzlers "Komödie der Verführung.* In: Festschrift for Herman Salinger, ed. Leland R. Phelps. Chapel Hill: University of North Carolina Press, 1977/1978.

SCHEIBLE, HARTMUT: *Arthur Schnitzler und die Aufklärung.* München: Wilhelm Fink Verlag, 1977, 124 p.

SHERMAN, MURRAY H.: *Schnitzler, Freud and The Murderer: The Limits of Insight in Psychoanalysis.* In: MAL, 10, iii/iv (1977).

SWALES, MARTIN: *Schnitzler's Tragi-Comedy: A Reading of "Das weite Land".* In: MAL, 10, iii/iv (1977).

WAGNER, RENATE: *Elisabeth Steinrück, geb. Gussmann, Olga Schnitzlers Schwester.* In: MAL, 10, iii/iv (1977).

INDEX OF SCHNITZLER TITLES

INDEX OF SUBJECTS & THEMES

INDEX OF PERSONAL NAMES

INDEX OF PERSONAL SUBJECT NAMES